Best of Chinese Cuisine
Home Style

SAM LEONG

CHINA INTERCONTINENTAL PRESS

图书在版编目（CIP）数据

上品中国菜—家常菜：英文 /（新加坡）梁兆基著
—北京：五洲传播出版社, 2011.3
ISBN 978-7-5085-2066-7

Ⅰ.①上… Ⅱ.①梁… Ⅲ.①菜谱－中国－英文 Ⅳ.①TS972.182

中国版本图书馆CIP数据核字(2011)第013983号

中华人民共和国国家版权局著作权合同登记号 图字01-2011-2374号

著　　　者：Sam Leong（新加坡）
出 版 人：荆孝敏
责任编辑：王莉
装帧设计：熊晓莹
设计制作：彼园文化（北京）有限公司

出版发行：五洲传播出版社
地　　址：北京市海淀区北三环中路31号凯奇大厦B座7层
邮　　编：100088
网　　址：www.cicc.org.cn
电　　话：010-82000227
印　　刷：恒美印务（广州）有限公司
开　　本：965x1028mm 1/16
印　　张：10.5
版　　次：2011年6月第1版 2015年6月第2次印刷
11800（平）

Contents

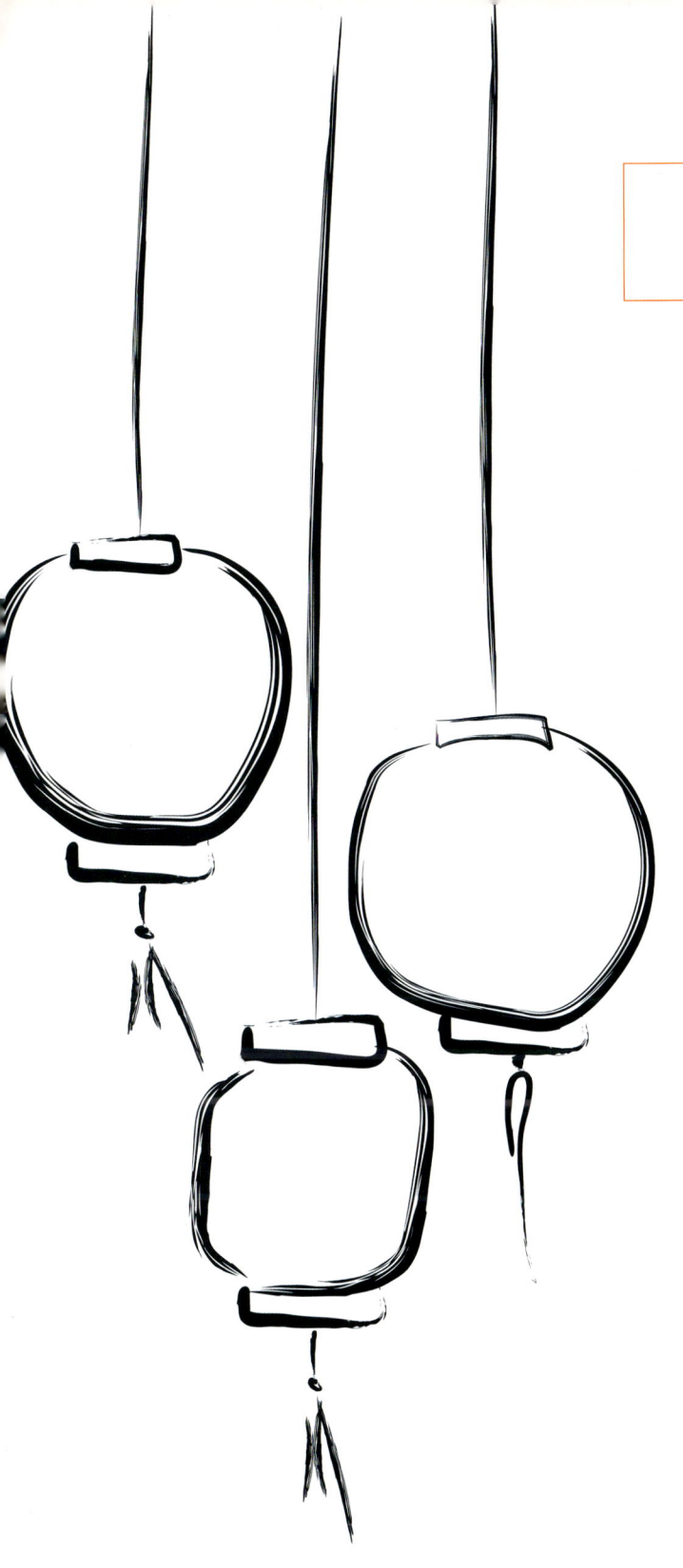

Foreword

When Sam asked me to write the foreword to this cookbook, I was only too glad to say yes. I have known Sam for more than 10 years and seen him grow from a young, earnest chef into today's celebrity masterchef. Yet in that time, one thing has never changed. He has always remained totally committed to his profession, challenging himself to continually come up with new ideas and standards.

Yet, as his professional stature rises, he has remained humble and affable. So this cookbook featuring recipes for everyday Chinese dishes best represents the Sam Leong I know: a man who is firmly rooted to his simple beginnings even though he now stands tall as one of Singapore's top chefs.

Unlike many celebrity chef cookbooks that serve better as trophies on a bookshelf because the recipes are too impractical for the home chef, this book is definitely one that will be well-thumbed. Dishes featured are designed for the home dinner table and can be whipped up easily in a home kitchen. And yet, they bear the imprint of a top-class chef.

The recipes speak from the heart, they speak of warmth and sincerity. This is a cookbook that anyone would be proud to have his name attached to. And one that everyone will be happy to keep.

Wong Ah Yoke

Straits Times restaurant critic

Introduction

I have been a chef for many years, but it was only when my wife, Forest, a chef by profession as well, started teaching cooking at cooking schools and community centres, that I gained an interest in doing the same.

Those who attended my cooking classes included working professionals and homemakers who wanted to learn more about Chinese cooking and more specifically, how they could whip up tasty and wholesome meals in a short time. It was the invaluable feedback I received from them that spurred me on to write this book on home-style Chinese cooking.

This collection of recipes is made up of dishes that can be prepared without fuss, yet with very tasty results. Where it does not make a noticeable difference to the final dish, I have used approximations instead of weights for the ingredients, to make the process of cooking easier. I have also taken shortcuts where applicable, such as using bottled sauces and ingredients, which can be found in most markets and supermarkets, to save on preparation time. Although I have included a recipe for chicken stock and used it frequently throughout the book, feel free either to prepare a larger batch and then freezing it in small quantities for use whenever you need it, or forgo the step altogether and purchase ready-made chicken stock. If using ready-made chicken stock, use unseasoned stock, or taste and adjust the seasoning of the dish accordingly.

Home cooking is really about cooking what you are comfortable with and what you like eating, so follow the recipes closely only if you are new to cooking. For those who are already experienced cooks, use these recipes merely as a guide and omit or substitute ingredients and steps as you please. The important thing is to enjoy the process of cooking and then sharing them with family or friends.

Some of these recipes are dishes which my grandmother and mother used to prepare for the family, and which I continue to treasure as my personal comfort foods today. I hope you will enjoy this collection of recipes and make them a part of your daily cooking routine!

Sam Leong

Soups

Pork Ball Soup with Seaweed 10

Double-boiled Black Chicken Soup with American Ginseng 12

White Bait & Clam Soup 14

Mussels in Ginger Soup 16

Double-boiled Stuffed Chicken & Ginseng Soup 18

Double-boiled Melon Soup with Seafood 20

Pork Rib Soup with Cabbage & Gingko Nuts 22

Double-boiled Coconut Soup with Baby Abalone 24

Dried Sole, Chinese Cabbage & Pork Soup 26

Pork Ball Soup with Seaweed Serves 4

Cooking oil *2 Tbsp*

White bait *a small handful*

Ginger *5 thin slices*

Spring onion (scallion) *1, chopped*

Chicken stock (page 159) *1 litre
(32 fl oz / 4 cups)*

Salt *1/2 tsp*

Sugar *1/2 tsp*

Ground white pepper *a pinch*

Dried Chinese seaweed *a small
handful*

Coriander leaves (cilantro) *1 sprig*

PORK BALLS

Minced pork shoulder *400 g
(14 1/3 oz)*

Minced pork fat *1 Tbsp*

Minced coriander stems (cilantro)
1 Tbsp

Water chestnuts *3, peeled and
minced*

Salt *1 tsp*

Sugar *1 tsp*

Egg white *1*

Ground white pepper *a pinch*

Sesame oil *a dash*

1. Start by preparing pork balls. Mix pork, pork fat, coriander stems and water chestnuts together in a mixing bowl. Add remaining ingredients and mix well. Scoop up a rounded teaspoonful of mixture and form into a ball. Repeat until mixture is used up.

2. Put pork balls on an oiled steaming tray and steam for about 5 minutes, or until pork balls are cooked.

3. Heat oil in a wok and add white bait, ginger and spring onion. Stir-fry until fragrant. Add chicken stock and bring to the boil. Season with salt, sugar and pepper.

4. Put pork balls and seaweed into a large bowl or individual serving bowls. Ladle soup over and garnish with coriander leaves. Serve hot.

NOTE Adding pork fat to the pork balls makes them flavourful and juicy. You can omit the pork fat for a healthier option, but the pork balls will not be as moist and tasty.

Double-boiled Black Chicken Soup with American Ginseng Serves 4

Black chicken *1, about 450 g (1 lb), cleaned*

American ginseng *1 piece, soaked in water for 10 minutes*

Chinese wolfberries *1 tsp*

Water *1 litre (32 fl oz / 4 cups)*

Salt *1/2 tsp*

Sugar *1/2 tsp*

Chinese cooking wine (*hua diao*) *a dash*

1. Put all the ingredients into the inner pot of a double-boiler, then put into the double-boiler and steam for 4 hours. If you do not have a double-boiler, put the ingredients into a heatproof pot, cover and steam for 4 hours.

2. Use a spoon to skim off the layer of fat from the soup. Transfer to a serving bowl and serve hot.

White Bait & Clam Soup Serves 4

White bait *300 g (11 oz)*

Clams *300 g (11 oz)*

Cooking oil *2 Tbsp*

Ginger *2 slices, shredded*

Chicken stock (page 159) *500 ml (16 fl oz / 2 cups)*

SEASONING
White miso paste *1 Tbsp*

Yellow bean sauce *1 Tbsp*

Light soy sauce *1/4 tsp*

Sugar *1/2 tsp*

Chinese cooking wine (*hua diao*) *a dash*

1. Bring a pot of water to the boil and poach white bait and clams briefly for about 5 seconds. Drain and set aside.

2. Heat oil in a wok. Add ginger and stir-fry until fragrant. Add chicken stock and ingredients for seasoning. Bring to the boil.

3. Add white bait and clams and return to the boil.

4. Ladle soup into bowls and serve hot.

Mussels in Ginger Soup Serves 4

Mussels *500 g (1 lb 1¹/₂ oz), cleaned*

Water *1 litre (32 fl oz / 4 cups)*

Salt *¹/₂ tsp*

Sugar *¹/₂ tsp*

Chinese cooking wine (*hua diao*)
   a dash

Ginger *5-cm (2-in) knob, peeled and
   shredded*

Coriander leaves (cilantro) *1 sprig*

1. Bring a pot of water to the boil and poach mussels very briefly for about 5 seconds. Drain.

2. Put mussels in a pot and add 1 litre (32 fl oz / 4 cups) water, salt, sugar, Chinese cooking wine and ginger. Bring to the boil.

3. Transfer to a bowl. Garnish with coriander leaves and serve hot.

NOTE You can use blue or green mussels or substitute the mussels with clams.

Double-boiled Stuffed Chicken & Ginseng Soup Serves 4

Glutinous rice *200 g (7 oz)*

Dried gingko nuts *8*

Dried lotus seeds *8*

Chinese red dates *3*

Spring chicken *1, about 450 g (1 lb), cleaned*

American ginseng *1 piece, soaked in water for 10 minutes*

Water *1 litre (32 fl oz / 4 cups)*

Salt *½ tsp*

Sugar *½ tsp*

Chinese cooking wine (*hua diao*) *a dash*

1. Start preparations up to 6 hours ahead. Soak glutinous rice in water and leave for 6 hours.

2. Prepare gingko nuts and lotus seeds. Soak them in warm water for 30 minutes. Use a wooden skewer to push the bitter shoot out from gingko nuts and lotus seeds.

3. Drain rice and mix with gingko nuts, lotus seeds and red dates. Stuff mixture into cavity of chicken. Use a skewer to seal opening of chicken.

4. Put chicken into the inner pot of a double-boiler. Add ginseng, water, salt, sugar and cooking wine. Put into the double-boiler and steam for 3 hours. If you do not have a double-boiler, put the ingredients into a heatproof pot, cover and steam for 3 hours.

5. Dish out and serve hot.

Double-boiled Melon Soup with Seafood Serves 4

Yellow cucumbers
  (*lao huang gua*) *2*

Salt *1 tsp*

Prawns (shrimps) *4*

Scallops *4*

Crabmeat *80 g (3 oz)*

Steamed dried scallops (page 159)
  4 scallops

Coriander leaves (cilantro) *1 sprig*

STOCK
Chicken stock (page 159) *800 ml
  (27 fl oz)*

Salt *1/2 tsp*

Chinese cooking wine (*hua diao*)
  1 tsp

Ground white pepper *a pinch*

1. Prepare yellow cucumbers. Cut in half crosswise, then use a spoon to scoop out the seeds. Slice the base of cucumbers to enable them to stand upright. Half-fill each cucumber half with water and add 1/4 tsp salt. Steam for 15 minutes until cucumber is slightly soft. Pour water away.

2. Bring a pot of water to the boil and lightly poach prawns and scallops. Peel prawns and dice. Dice scallops.

3. Divide prawns, scallops, crabmeat and steamed dried scallops with its liquid equally among the cucumber halves.

4. Combine ingredients for stock in a pot and bring to the boil. Pour hot stock into yellow cucumber halves and place in a steamer for 15 minutes.

5. Garnish as desired and serve hot.

Pork Rib Soup with Cabbage & Gingko Nuts Serves 4

Dried gingko nuts *10*

Pork ribs *500 g (1 lb 1¹/₂ oz),*
cut in 4-cm (1¹/₂-in) pieces

Water *3 litres (96 fl oz / 12 cups)*

Salt *¹/₂ tsp*

Sugar *¹/₂ tsp*

Ground white pepper *a pinch*

Chinese cabbage *300 g (11 oz),*
cut in small pieces

Black fungus *10 g (¹/₃ oz), soaked*
in water for 30 minutes

Dried mandarin peel *2.5-cm (1-in)*
square

GARNISH

Chinese wolfberries *1 tsp*

Coriander leaves (cilantro) *1 sprig*

1. Soak gingko nuts in warm water for 30 minutes, then use a wooden skewer to push the bitter shoot out.

2. Bring a pot of water to the boil and poach pork ribs to remove any surface scum. Drain.

3. Put all ingredients, except garnish, in a pot and bring to the boil over high heat. Boil for 20 minutes, then lower heat and simmer for 1 hour until liquid is reduced by half and pork ribs are tender.

4. Ladle soup into bowls and garnish with Chinese wolfberries and coriander. Serve hot.

Double-boiled Coconut Soup with Baby Abalone Serves 4

Canned baby abalones *4*

Dried lotus seeds *8*

Chicken stock (page 159) *1 litre (32 fl oz / 4 cups)*

Salt *1/2 tsp*

Sugar *1/2 tsp*

Chinese cooking wine (*hua diao*) *a dash*

Fragrant Solomon seal rhizome (*yu zhu*) *10 g (1/3 oz)*

Old (mature) coconuts *2, halved*

1. Start preparations at least 5 hours ahead. Steam or boil unopened can of abalones for 3 hours (*see* Note on page 66).

2. Soak lotus seeds in warm water for 30 minutes, then use a wooden skewer to push the bitter shoot out.

3. Put chicken stock into a pot and add salt, sugar and Chinese cooking wine. Bring to the boil.

4. Place 1 abalone, 2 lotus seeds and Solomon seal rhizome into each coconut half. Place coconut halves into bowls, so they stand upright. Ladle stock into coconut halves and place in a steamer for 2 hours.

5. Remove coconut halves from steamer and serve hot.

NOTE If mature coconuts are not available, use the young Thai coconuts available from the chiller section of some supermarkets. Reserve the coconut water from these young Thai coconuts for a cooling drink.

Dried Sole, Chinese Cabbage & Pork Soup Serves 4

Dried sole *1/2 piece*

Pork shoulder *100 g (3 1/2 oz), thinly sliced*

Salt *a pinch*

Sugar *a pinch*

Sesame oil *a dash*

Egg white *1/2*

Corn flour (cornstarch) *5 Tbsp*

Cooking oil *for deep-frying*

Chinese cabbage *200 g (7 oz), chopped*

Dried Chinese mushrooms *5, soaked to soften, then sliced*

STOCK

Chicken stock (page 159) *750 ml (24 fl oz / 3 cups)*

Salt *1/2 tsp*

Sugar *1/2 tsp*

Sesame oil *a dash*

Chinese cooking wine (*hua diao*) *a dash*

1. Preheat oven to 150°C (300°F) and bake dried sole for 10–12 minutes until it is brown and crisp.

2. Meanwhile, marinate pork with salt, sugar, sesame oil and egg white and leave for 10 minutes. Coat with corn flour.

3. Heat oil for deep-frying and deep-fry pork until brown and crisp. Drain and set aside.

4. Put ingredients for stock into a pot and bring to the boil. Lower heat to a simmer.

5. Crush baked dried sole and add to stock. Simmer for 5 minutes, then add cabbage, mushrooms and deep-fried pork. Increase heat to high and boil until cabbage is soft.

6. Ladle into bowls and serve hot.

Fish &
Seafood

Crispy Prawn Balls with Cheese 30

Wok-fried Snakehead with Ginger & Spring-Onion 32

Deep-fried Fish in Sweet & Sour Sauce 34

Steamed Fish Head with Pickled Chillies & Black Beans 36

Deep-fried Fish with Homemade Soy Sauce 38

Crispy Cod Fillet with Mango Salsa 40

Poached Fish Fillet in Barley Broth 42

Steamed Whole Fish in Homemade Soy Sauce 44

Braised Sea Cucumber with Spicy Meat Sauce 46

Wok-fried Clams with Basil 48

Stir-fried Oysters with Spring-Onion & Garlic 50

Stir-fried Spicy Prawns with Pickled Red Bell Peppers 52

Steamed Tiger Prawns with Minced Garlic 54

Steamed Crab with Egg White 56

Crabs in Chilli-Orange Sauce 58

Stuffed Crispy Crab Shells 60

Stuffed Steamed Squid in Lime-Chicken Stock 62

Four-Treasure Pot with Dried Scallops, Fish Maw,
    Sea Cucumber & Abalone 64

Abalone & Broccoli with Dried Scallop Sauce 66

Crispy Prawn Balls with Cheese Serves 4

Spinach leaves *a handful*

Prawns (shrimps) *80 g (3 oz)*

Cheddar cheese *4 small cubes, each about 20 g (²/₃ oz)*

Cooking oil *for deep-frying*

Sliced white bread *6 slices, crust removed and cut into small cubes*

SEASONING (COMBINED)

Salt *¹/₄ tsp*

Sugar *¹/₂ tsp*

Sesame oil *¹/₂ tsp*

Egg white *¹/₂*

Corn flour (cornstarch) *¹/₄ tsp*

Ground white pepper *¹/₂ tsp*

1. Bring a pot of water to the boil and blanch spinach leaves until just wilted. Drain well, then mince.

2. Peel and devein prawns. Rinse, then chop using the spine of a cleaver until mixture is pasty. Mix prawn paste with spinach and ingredients for seasoning. Divide mixture into 8 portions.

3. Roll each portion into a ball, then press a cube of cheese into each ball. Reshape balls to enclose cheese.

4. Heat oil for deep-frying over medium heat.

5. Coat prawn balls with bread cubes, pressing gently so bread sticks to prawn balls. Deep-fry in batches over medium heat until golden brown and crisp. Takes about 3 minutes.

6. Drain well and serve hot.

NOTE It will be easier to slice the bread into small cubes if it is frozen beforehand.

Wok-fried Snakehead with Ginger & Spring Onion Serves 4

Snakehead (*sang yu*) fillet *500 g (1 lb 1¹/₂ oz)*

Salt *a pinch*

Sugar *a pinch*

Sesame oil *a dash*

Corn flour (cornstarch) *1 tsp*

Egg white *1*

Cooking oil *2 Tbsp*

Spring onions (scallions) *3, cut into short lengths*

Ginger *5-cm (2-in) knob, peeled and sliced*

Garlic *2–3 cloves, peeled and thinly sliced*

SEASONING (COMBINED)

Chicken stock (page 159) or water *3 Tbsp*

Oyster sauce *1 tsp*

Light soy sauce *¹/₂ tsp*

Sugar *¹/₂ tsp*

Ground white pepper *a pinch*

Chinese cooking wine (*hua diao*) *a dash*

Corn flour (cornstarch) *¹/₂ tsp, mixed with 2 tsp water*

1. Marinate fish with salt, sugar, sesame oil, corn flour and egg white.

2. Heat oil in a wok over medium heat. Add fish and stir-fry until cooked. Remove and drain.

3. Using the same wok, stir-fry spring onion, ginger and garlic until fragrant. Add fish and ingredients for seasoning and stir-fry lightly.

4. Dish out and serve hot.

Deep-fried Fish in Sweet & Sour Sauce Serves 4

Grouper *1, about 1 kg (2 lb 3 oz)*

Egg *1, beaten*

Salt *¼ tsp*

Ground star anise *a pinch*

Cooking oil *for deep-frying*

Corn flour (cornstarch) *600 g (1 lb 5⅓ oz)*

Red and green capsicums (bell peppers) *1 each, small, cored and diced*

Canned sweet corn kernels *⅓ cup*

Tomato sauce *10 Tbsp*

SWEET AND SOUR SAUCE

Water *250 ml (8 fl oz / 1 cup)*

Sugar *150 g (5⅓ oz)*

Brown sugar *100 g (3½ oz)*

Salt *1 tsp or to taste*

White vinegar *125 ml (4 fl oz / ½ cup)*

1. Prepare sweet and sour sauce. Combine all ingredients for sauce in a pan, except vinegar. Bring to the boil, stirring until sugar is dissolved. Leave to cool before stirring in vinegar.

2. Fillet fish leaving tail on. Make criss cross cuts on flesh, so fish will curl up when cooked. Marinate fish with egg, salt and ground star anise for 20 minutes.

3. Heat oil for deep-frying. Coat marinated fish with corn flour and lower into hot oil. Deep-fry for 5 minutes until cooked and golden brown. Remove and drain well. Place on a serving dish.

4. Reheat 1 Tbsp oil in a wok. Add capsicums and sweet corn and stir-fry lightly. Add sweet and sour sauce and tomato sauce and bring to the boil.

5. Pour over fish and serve immediately.

Steamed Fish Head with Pickled Chillies & Black Beans Serves 4

Song fish head *800 g (1³/₄ lb)*

Chicken stock (page 159) *80 ml (2¹/₂ fl oz / ¹/₃ cup)*

Chinese cooking wine (*hua diao*) *1 Tbsp*

Ground white pepper *a pinch*

Pickled red chillies (page 160) *10 Tbsp*

Fermented black beans *1 Tbsp, soaked in water for 5 minutes*

Spring onion (scallion) *1, chopped*

Cooking oil *3 Tbsp*

Homemade soy sauce (page 160) *3 Tbsp*

1. Clean fish head and chop into pieces.

2. Place fish head on a steaming plate and add chicken stock and Chinese cooking wine. Season with pepper, then spoon pickled red chilli and black beans evenly over fish. Steam for 10 minutes or until fish is cooked.

3. Sprinkle spring onion over fish.

4. Heat oil in a wok and pour over fish. Do the same with homemade soy sauce. Serve hot.

NOTE Pickled red chillies are available in jars from some supermarkets. If unavailable, prepare your own using the recipe on page 160.

Deep-fried Fish with Homemade Soy Sauce Serves 4

Marbled goby or red grouper *1, about 800 g (1³/₄ lb)*

Cooking oil *for deep-frying*

Spring onions (scallions) *2, white part only, shredded*

Homemade soy sauce (page 160) *200 ml (7 fl oz)*

Coriander leaves (cilantro) *1 sprig*

Red chilli *1, seeded and thinly sliced*

1. Clean fish and butterfly it. Do this by inserting the tip of a very sharp knife into the belly of the fish near the tail. Slide the knife in until you feel the spine and slice along the length of the fish. Do not cut through the spine. Open the fish up, so it sits flat.

2. Heat oil for deep-frying in a large wok. When oil is very hot, gently lower fish into oil, flesh side down. Deep-fry for 3 minutes until fish is crisp and brown.

3. Remove and drain fish. Place fish on a serving plate and top with spring onions.

4. Heat 2 Tbsp oil in a wok and pour over spring onions. Do the same with homemade soy sauce. Garnish with coriander leaves and red chilli and serve.

Crispy Cod Fillet with Mango Salsa Serves 4

Cod fish fillets *4, each about 200 g (7 oz)*

Cooking oil *for deep-frying*

Thai sweet chilli sauce

MANGO SALSA

Ripe mango *200 g (7 oz), peeled and diced*

Shallots *3, peeled and minced*

Mint leaves *10 leaves, minced*

Thai sweet chilli sauce *3 Tbsp*

1. Start by preparing mango salsa. Toss all the ingredients together, then refrigerate until chilled. The mango salsa must be consumed within a few hours of preparation.

2. Make criss cross cuts on fish fillets, so they will curl up when cooked. Heat oil for deep-frying and deep-fry fish over high heat until fish is crisp and golden brown.

3. Serve fish on a bed of mango salsa with Thai sweet chilli sauce on the side.

Poached Fish Fillet in Barley Broth Serves 4

Barley *40 g (1¹/₂ oz)*

Thai fragrant rice *40 g (1¹/₂ oz),*
  crushed

Cooking oil *2 Tbsp*

Green asparagus *100 g (3¹/₂ oz),*
  chopped

Preserved vegetable (*xue cai*)
  2 Tbsp

Salt *to taste*

Ground white pepper *to taste*

Grouper fillet *300 g (11 oz),*
  thinly sliced

Sugar *¹/₂ tsp*

Sesame oil *a dash*

Corn flour (cornstarch) *¹/₂ tsp*

Egg white *1*

Fried cruller (*you tiao*) *1 stick, sliced*

1. Put barley in a pot with 2 litres (64 fl oz / 8 cups) water and simmer over low heat for 45 minutes until barley is soft.

2. Put rice in a pot with 1 litre (32 fl oz / 4 cups) water and simmer over low heat for 45 minutes until grains are soft and porridge-like.

3. Heat oil in a wok and add barley and porridge, asparagus and preserved vegetable. Bring to the boil and season to taste with salt and pepper.

4. Marinate fish with ¹/₂ tsp salt, sugar, sesame oil, corn flour, and egg white.

5. Add fish to wok one slice at a time and stir gently for 3 minutes until fish is cooked.

6. Ladle into bowls and garnish with fried crullers. Serve hot.

Steamed Whole Fish in Homemade Soy Sauce Serves 4

Grouper *1, about 1 kg (2 lb 3 oz), cleaned*

Spring onions (scallions) *3, white part only, shredded*

Cooking oil *2 Tbsp*

Homemade soy sauce (page 160) *200 ml (7 fl oz)*

GARNISH

Coriander leaves (cilantro) *1 sprig*

Red chilli *1, shredded*

Ginger *1 small knob, peeled and shredded*

1. Place a chopstick on a steaming plate and place grouper on top. This will allow the grouper to cook more evenly. Place in a steamer and steam for 8 minutes until cooked. To test if fish is cooked, insert a chopstick into the thickest part of fish. The chopstick should go through easily. If not, steam for another few minutes.

2. Top fish with spring onions.

3. Heat oil in a wok and spoon over spring onions. Do the same with homemade soy sauce.

4. Garnish with coriander leaves, chilli and ginger. Serve immediately.

Braised Sea Cucumber with Spicy Meat Sauce Serves 4

BRAISED SEA CUCUMBER

Ready-prepared sea cucumber *200 g (7 oz), cut into 4-cm (1¹/₂-in) pieces*

Cooking oil *2 Tbsp*

Spring onion (scallion) *¹/₂, chopped*

Ginger *2 slices*

Chicken stock (page 159) *500 ml (16 fl oz / 2 cups)*

Light soy sauce *¹/₂ tsp*

Oyster sauce *¹/₂ tsp*

SPICY MEAT SAUCE

Cooking oil *2 Tbsp*

Spring onion (scallion) *1, chopped*

Red chilli *1, chopped*

Garlic *3 cloves, peeled and minced*

Shallots *3, peeled and minced*

Minced pork shoulder *80 g (3 oz)*

Chicken stock (page 159) or water *80 ml (2¹/₂ fl oz / ¹/₃ cup)*

Hot bean sauce *3 tsp*

Sugar *¹/₂ tsp*

Oyster sauce *1 tsp*

Sesame oil *1 tsp*

Dark soy sauce *a dash*

Chinese cooking wine (*hua tiao*) *a dash*

Corn flour (cornstarch) *¹/₂ tsp, mixed with 2 tsp water*

1. Soak sea cucumber in hot water for 2 minutes. Drain and set aside.

2. Heat oil in a wok and stir-fry spring onion and ginger until fragrant. Add chicken stock, light soy sauce and oyster sauce and bring to the boil.

3. Add sea cucumber, lower heat and simmer gently for 30 minutes until sea cucumber is brown and has absorbed all the flavours of the stock. Set sea cucumber aside. Discard other ingredients.

4. Prepare spicy meat sauce. Heat oil in a wok and sauté spring onion, chilli, garlic, shallots and minced pork until fragrant. Add chicken stock or water, sea cucumber and remaining ingredients for sauce, except corn flour. Bring to the boil, then stir in corn flour mixture to thicken sauce.

5. Dish out and garnish as desired. Serve hot.

Wok-fried Clams with Basil Serves 4

Clams *1 kg (2 lb 3 oz), rinsed*

Cooking oil *2 Tbsp*

Garlic *5 cloves, peeled and minced*

Red chillies *2, sliced*

Spring onion (scallion) *1, chopped*

Chicken stock (page 159) or water
  100 ml (3¹/₂ oz)

Oyster sauce *2 Tbsp*

Light soy sauce *¹/₄ tsp*

Sugar *¹/₂ tsp*

Dark soy sauce *a dash*

Sesame oil *¹/₂ tsp*

Maggi seasoning *¹/₄ tsp*

Basil leaves *a handful*

Corn flour (cornstarch) *¹/₂ tsp,
  mixed 2 tsp water*

1. Bring a large pot of water to the boil and poach clams for 10 seconds. Drain.

2. Heat oil in a wok and add garlic, chillies and spring onion. Stir-fry until fragrant, then quickly add clams and stir-fry until fragrant.

3. Add all remaining ingredients except basil and corn flour and mix well.

4. Add basil leaves and thicken sauce with corn flour mixture. Dish out and serve immediately.

Stir-fried Oysters with Spring Onion & Garlic Serves 4

Cooking oil *2 Tbsp*

Garlic *1 clove, peeled and minced*

Shallot *1, peeled and minced*

Ginger *1-cm (1/2-in) knob, peeled and minced*

Fresh small oysters *300 g (11 oz)*

Spring onion (scallion) *1, sliced*

Red chillies *2, sliced*

Fermented black beans *1 tsp, soaked in water for 10 minutes*

Yellow bean sauce *1/2 tsp*

Oyster sauce *1 tsp*

Dark soy sauce *a dash*

Chinese cooking wine (*hua diao*) *a dash*

Sugar *1/2 tsp*

Chicken stock (page 159) or water *80 ml (21/2 fl oz / 1/3 cup)*

Corn flour (cornstarch) *1/2 tsp, mixed with 2 tsp water*

1. Heat oil in a wok and add garlic, shallots and ginger. Stir-fry until fragrant.

2. Add remaining ingredients, except corn flour, and stir-fry for 1–2 minutes until oysters are cooked.

3. Add corn flour mixture to thicken sauce. Dish out and serve.

NOTE Oysters can be substituted with clams in this recipe.

Stir-fried Spicy Prawns with Pickled Red Bell Peppers Serves 4

Cooking oil *for deep-frying*

Spring onion (scallion) *1, chopped*

Garlic *3 cloves, peeled and minced*

Shallots *3, peeled and minced*

Pickled red bell peppers (*see* Note) *80 g (3 oz)*

Corn flour (cornstarch) *¹/₂ tsp, mixed with 2 tsp water*

PRAWNS

Prawns (shrimps) *8*

Salt *a pinch*

Sugar *a pinch*

Egg white *¹/₂*

Sesame oil *a dash*

Corn flour (cornstarch) *¹/₈ tsp*

SEASONING (COMBINED)

Chicken stock (page 159) or water *80 ml (2¹/₂ fl oz / ¹/₃ cup)*

Hot bean paste *3 tsp*

Sugar *¹/₂ tsp*

Oyster sauce *1 tsp*

Sesame oil *1 tsp*

Dark soy sauce *a dash*

Chinese cooking wine (*hua diao*) *a dash*

1. Prepare prawns. Peel prawns, then make a slit down the back of each one. Remove vein and rinse. Marinate with salt, sugar, egg white, sesame oil and corn flour. Leave for 10 minutes.

2. Heat oil for deep-frying over medium heat. Add prawns and cook for about 20 seconds. Remove prawns and drain away oil.

3. Reheat 2 Tbsp oil in the wok and stir-fry spring onion, garlic and shallots until fragrant. Add prawns and pickled bell peppers Stir-fry lightly.

4. Add ingredients for seasoning and thicken with corn flour mixture. Dish out and serve hot.

NOTE Pickled red bell peppers are available in jars from the supermarket. Refer to the Glossary for more on pickled red bell peppers.

Steamed Tiger Prawns with Minced Garlic Serves 4

Freshwater prawns (shrimps) *4, each about 100 g (3¹/₂ oz)*

Glass vermicelli *a small handful, soaked in water for 30 minutes*

Garlic *2 heads, peeled and minced*

Crispy minced garlic (page 161) *1 Tbsp*

Salt *¹/₄ tsp*

Corn flour (cornstarch) *¹/₂ tsp, mixed with 2 tsp water*

Cooking oil *4 Tbsp*

Spring onion (scallion) *1, chopped*

Homemade soy sauce (page 160) *3 Tbsp*

1. Remove prawn heads and trim off legs. Leave shell and tails on prawns. Cut prawns in half lengthwise, then arrange on a steaming plate.

2. Drain vermicelli and dip into hot water for 10 seconds. Drain well and put on the steaming plate with prawns.

3. Combine minced garlic, crispy minced garlic, salt, corn flour mixture and 2 Tbsp oil, then pour over prawns. Steam for 4 minutes or until prawns are cooked. Garnish with spring onion.

4. Reheat 2 Tbsp oil in a wok and pour over spring onion. Do the same with homemade soy sauce. Serve immediately.

Steamed Crab with Egg White

Serves 4

Crabs *2, each about 500 g
(1 lb 1 1/2 oz)*

Ginger *5-cm (2-in) knob, peeled and
shredded*

Cooking oil *2 Tbsp*

Chives *a small bunch, chopped*

Homemade soy sauce (page 160)
125 ml (4 fl oz / 1/2 cup)

SEASONING (COMBINED)

Egg whites *3*

Water *5 Tbsp*

Salt *1/2 tsp*

Sugar *1/2 tsp*

Sesame oil *a dash*

Ground white pepper *a dash*

1. Pull off top shells and clean crabs. Chop into pieces, then rinse and drain well. Place on a heatproof plate.

2. Pour ingredients for seasoning over crabs. Sprinkle shredded ginger over and place in a steamer for 6 minutes until crabs are cooked.

3. Reheat homemade soy sauce and pour over crabs. Garnish with chives and serve hot.

Crabs in Chilli-Orange Sauce

Serves 4

Sri Lankan crabs 2, *each about 800 g (1³/₄ lb)*

Cooking oil *2 Tbsp*

Chicken stock (page 159) *300 ml (10 fl oz / 1¹/₄ cups)*

Corn flour (cornstarch) *¹/₂ tsp, mixed with 2 tsp water*

Eggs *2, beaten*

Coriander leaves (cilantro) *1 sprig*

Orange *1, peeled and segmented*

CHILLI-ORANGE SAUCE

Red chillies *50 g (1²/₃ oz), stalks removed*

Bird's eye chillies (*chilli padi*) *15 g (¹/₂ oz), stalks removed*

Dried chillies *15 g (¹/₂ oz), soaked to soften and drained*

Cooking oil *as needed*

Dried prawns (shrimps) *15 g (¹/₂ oz), soaked to soften*

Garlic *15 g (¹/₂ oz), peeled*

Shallots *15 g (¹/₂ oz), peeled*

Galangal *15 g (¹/₂ oz), peeled*

Torch ginger bud *25 g (1 oz), use pink bud only*

Chicken seasoning powder *10 g (¹/₃ oz)*

Tomato sauce *4¹/₂ Tbsp*

Orange cordial *300 ml (10 fl oz / 1¹/₄ cups)*

1. Start by preparing the chili-orange sauce. Put fresh and dried chillies in a blender with a little oil to help make the blending easier. Blend into a smooth paste and set aside. Repeat to blend dried prawns, adding oil as necessary, then set aside. Blend garlic, shallots, galangal and torch ginger bud together, adding oil as necessary. (This may seem like a very oily sauce, but the oil can be drained off after the sauce is cooked.)

2. Heat 2 Tbsp oil in a wok and stir-fry blended dried prawns over low heat until crisp and fragrant. Set aside.

3. Heat another 2 Tbsp oil in the wok and stir-fry galangal mixture until fragrant. Set aside.

4. Heat another 2 Tbsp oil in the wok and stir-fry blended chillies over low heat for at least 10 minutes until chillies are cooked.
   Add galangal mixture and dried prawns. When mixture starts to bubble, stir in chicken seasoning, tomato sauce and orange cordial. Mix well and set aside.

5. Pull off top shells and clean crabs. Chop into pieces, then rinse and drain well. Place in a steamer for 5 minutes until crabs change colour and are cooked. Set aside.

6. Heat 2 Tbsp oil in a wok and add chicken stock and chilli-orange sauce. Add crabs and mix well. Bring sauce to the boil, then thicken with corn flour mixture and turn off heat.

7. Add eggs and mix slowly. Eggs will cook in the residual heat.

8. Dish out and garnish with coriander leaves. Serve hot.

NOTE To save time when you next prepare this dish, you can whip up a larger batch of chilli-orange sauce and keep it refrigerated for up to 1 month. Due to the addition of oil for blending the ingredients, the resulting chilli-orange sauce may be rather oily. Allow the cooked sauce to sit for a while until the oil separates. Drain the layer of oil away and reserve it for flavouring other dishes, if desired.

Stuffed Crispy Crab Shells Serves 4

Flower crabs *4*

Prawns (shrimps) *200 g (7 oz)*

Minced coriander (cilantro) stems
1/2 Tbsp

Water chestnuts *3, peeled and
chopped*

Breadcrumbs *4 Tbsp*

Cooking oil *for deep-frying*

Thai sweet chilli sauce *4 Tbsp*

SEASONING (COMBINED)
Salt *1/2 tsp*

Sugar *1 tsp*

Sesame oil *1/2 tsp*

Egg white *1/2*

Corn flour (cornstarch) *1/2 tsp*

Ground white pepper *1/2 tsp*

1. Prepare crabs. Wash top shells and set aside to dry. Place crabs in a steamer and steam for 5 minutes. Leave to cool slightly, then remove meat.

2. Peel and devein prawns. Rinse, then chop prawns using the spine of a cleaver until mixture is pasty. Combine prawn paste with crab meat, coriander stems, water chestnuts and ingredients for seasoning. Mix well.

3. Fill cleaned top shells with mixture, then coat with breadcrumbs.

4. Heat oil for deep-frying over medium heat. Lower stuffed crab shells into hot oil and deep-fry for about 5 minutes until golden brown and cooked. Remove and drain well.

5. Serve with Thai sweet chilli sauce.

Stuffed Steamed Squid in Lime-Chicken Stock
Serves 4

Baby squid *4, each about 125 g (4¹/₂ oz)*

Cooking oil *1 Tbsp*

STUFFING (COMBINED)

Minced pork shoulder *200 g (7 oz)*

Minced pork fat *1 Tbsp*

Minced coriander (cilantro) stems
  1 Tbsp

Water chestnuts *3, peeled and minced*

Salt *¹/₂ tsp*

Sugar *¹/₂ tsp*

Egg white *1*

Ground white pepper *a pinch*

Sesame oil *a dash*

LIME-CHICKEN STOCK

Chicken stock (page 159) *250 ml
  (8 fl oz / 1 cup)*

Lime juice *3 Tbsp*

Fish sauce *1 tsp*

Sugar *1 tsp*

Minced garlic *2 tsp*

Minced coriander (cilantro) stems *2 tsp*

Minced red chilli *¹/₄ tsp*

Minced bird eye chilli (optional)
  ¹/₄ tsp

GARNISH

Large lime *1, sliced*

Coriander leaves (cilantro) *1 sprig*

1. Clean baby squid. Pull out the head and the innards will follow. Remove the transparent quill and wash the squid tube. Peel off the purplish skin and cut away the wings. In this recipe, we only need the squid tubes. You can add the tentacles and wings to stir-fries, if desired. Be sure to cut away the eyes, beak and ink sac before using the head and tentacles.

2. Fill squid tubes with stuffing, then seal opening of tubes by sewing with string or using bamboo skewers.

3. Steam stuffed squid for 6 minutes, or until cooked. Remove string or bamboo skewers and cut squid into thick rounds. Arrange on a serving plate.

4. Heat oil in a wok and add ingredients for stock. Bring to the boil and pour over squid.

5. Garnish with slices of lime and coriander leaves.

NOTE Adding pork fat to the stuffing makes it flavourful and juicy. You can omit the pork fat for a healthier option, but the stuffing will not be as moist and tasty.

Four-Treasure Pot with Dried Scallops, Fish Maw, Sea Cucumber & Abalone Serves 4

Dried fish maw *4 pieces*

Black hair moss *a small handful*

Ginger *1 slice*

Canned baby abalones (*see* Note) *4 pieces*

Braised sea cucumber (page 48) *1 recipe*

Steamed dried scallops (page 159) *4 pieces*

Broccoli *100 g (3¹/₂ oz), cut into florets*

Cooking oil

Chicken stock (page 159) *435 ml (14 fl oz / 1³/₄ cups)*

Oyster sauce *2 Tbsp*

Dark soy sauce *2 tsp*

Sugar *2 tsp*

Chinese cooking wine (*hua diao*) *2 tsp*

Corn flour (cornstarch) *2 tsp, mixed with 1 Tbsp water*

1. Prepare dried fish maw a few days ahead. Bring a pot of water to the boil, then add fish maw. Remove from heat, cover and leave overnight. The following day, drain and soak fish maw in water for 12 hours. Repeat the process of boiling and soaking fish maw until it is completely soft. Takes 2–3 days. Be careful not to let fish maw come into contact with oil during this process or it will spoil.

2. On the day of cooking, steam or boil unopened can of abalones for 3 hours (*see* Note).

3. Soak black hair moss in hot water for 30 minutes. Drain, then soak in a fresh change of hot water, along with a slice of ginger. Place in a steamer and steam for 20 minutes until black hair moss is soft. Drain.

4. Divide fish maw, hair moss, abalones, sea cucumber, dried scallops and broccoli among 4 steaming bowls. Place in a steamer and steam for 5 minutes.

5. Meanwhile, heat oil in a wok and add chicken stock. Bring to the boil and season with oyster sauce, dark soy sauce, sugar and Chinese cooking wine. When stock returns to the boil, stir in corn flour mixture to thicken stock lightly.

6. Ladle stock into bowls and serve immediately.

NOTE A can of baby abalones may contain up to 10 pieces. For such cans, steam or boil for 3 hours. Use the remaining abalones in other recipes. If using larger abalones, the cans may contain only 2 or 3 pieces. Larger abalones will require a longer cooking time of 4–5 hours. Adjust the steaming/boiling time as necessary.

Abalone & Broccoli with Dried Scallop Sauce Serves 4

Canned baby abalones (*see* Note, page 66) *4 pieces*

Broccoli *1 small head, cut into florets*

Cooking oil *2 Tbsp*

Chicken stock (page 159) *125 ml (4 fl oz / 1/2 cup)*

Steamed dried scallops (page 159) *10 pieces*

Oyster sauce *2 tsp*

Dark soy sauce *a dash*

Chinese cooking wine (*hua diao*) *a dash*

Sugar *1/2 tsp*

Corn flour (cornstarch) *1 tsp, mixed with 2 tsp water*

1. Prepare canned abalones a few hours ahead. Steam or boil unopened can of abalones for 3 hours.

2. Place abalones and broccoli on a steaming plate and steam for 5 minutes.

3. Meanwhile, heat oil in a wok and add chicken stock and dried scallops. Bring to the boil and season with oyster sauce, dark soy sauce, Chinese cooking wine and sugar. When stock returns to the boil, stir in corn flour mixture to thicken stock lightly.

4. Pour stock over abalone and broccoli and serve hot.

Meat &
Poultry

Braised Pork Leg 10

Fried Pork Ribs with Sweet & Sour Orange Sauce 12

Braised Pork Belly with Pickled Bamboo Shoot 14

Braised Pork Trotters & Peanuts 16

My Grandmother's Steamed Minced Pork Petites with
  Salted Egg Yolk 18

Sliced Pork with Garlic Vinaigrette Sauce 80

Steamed Minced Pork with Sichuan Pickled Cabbage 82

Crispy Pork Ribs Coated with Five-Spice Powder 84

Slow-poached Beef in Sweet Soy Sauce 86

Pan-seared Beef Rolls with Black Pepper Sauce 88

Slow-stewed Beef Cubes with Radish 90

Poached Boneless Chicken with Warm Ginger Sauce 92

My Grandmother's Steamed Chicken with Fermented Bean Curd 94

Braised Pork Leg Serves 4

Pork leg *1, about 600 g (1 lb 5¹/₃ oz)*

Water *2 litres (64 fl oz / 8 cups)*

Pickled leeks *2*

Dried mandarin peel *2.5-cm (1-in) piece*

Spring onion (scallion) *1*

Ginger *5-cm (2-in) knob, peeled*

Star anise *2*

Bay leaves *2*

Dried chillies *2*

Chinese red dates *15*

Light soy sauce *3 Tbsp*

Seafood sauce *1 Tbsp*

Dark soy sauce *¹/₂ tsp*

Sugar *1 Tbsp*

1. Using a kitchen torch, lightly torch pork leg to remove any hair on skin. Alternatively, burn it using an open flame on the stove top. Bring a large pot of water to the boil and poach pork leg for 5 minutes to remove any smell and surface scum. Drain well.

2. Put pork leg and remaining ingredients into a pot. Simmer over low heat for 1–1¹/₂ hours until pork leg is tender and stock has thickened slightly. Alternatively, use a pressure cooker to reduce the cooking time to 30 minutes.

3. Remove pork leg and debone if desired. Strain sauce. Garnish, if desired, and serve hot.

NOTE Pickled leek is available in jars from the supermarket.

Fried Pork Ribs with Sweet & Sour Orange Sauce Serves 4

Pork ribs *400 g (14¹/₃ oz),*
  chopped into small pieces

Water *1.5 litres (48 fl oz / 6 cups)*

Cooking oil *for deep-frying*

Corn flour (cornstarch) *200 g (7 oz)*

White sesame seeds *1 tsp, toasted*

Green apple *1, cored and cut into wedges*
  just before serving

SEASONING AND AROMATICS

Oyster sauce *2 tsp*

Sugar *1 tsp*

Dark soy sauce *¹/₈ tsp*

Chinese cooking wine (*hua diao*) *3 tsp*

Ginger *3 slices*

Spring onion (scallion) *¹/₂*

Dried chillies *5*

Red chillies *2*

Star anise *1*

Bay leaf *1*

SWEET AND SOUR ORANGE SAUCE

Freshly squeezed orange juice
  100 ml (3¹/₂ fl oz)

Tomato sauce *5 Tbsp*

Sugar *3 Tbsp*

Brown sugar *3 Tbsp*

Salt *2 tsp*

White vinegar *4 Tbsp*

1. Bring a pot of water to the boil and poach pork ribs lightly to remove any surface scum. Drain well.

2. Put pork ribs in a pot. Add water and seasoning and aromatics and simmer over low heat for 1¹/₂ hours until meat is tender. Drain ribs and discard contents of pot.

3. Put ingredients for sweet and sour orange sauce in a pot and bring to the boil, stirring until sugar is dissolved. Taste and adjust seasoning if necessary. Remove from heat.

4. Heat oil for deep-frying. Coat ribs with corn flour, then lower into hot oil and deep-fry until brown and crisp. Drain well.

5. Toss pork ribs in sweet and sour orange sauce, then sprinkle with sesame seeds. Serve garnished with green apple wedges.

Braised Pork Belly with Pickled Bamboo Shoot Serves 4

Pork belly *400 g (14¹/₃ oz)*

Light soy sauce *1 Tbsp*

Cooking oil *for deep-frying*

Chicken stock (page 159) *1.5 litres (48 fl oz / 6 cups)*

Corn flour (cornstarch) *¹/₂ tsp, mixed with 2 tsp water*

Pickled bamboo shoot with chilli *150 g (5¹/₃ oz)*

SEASONING AND AROMATICS

Chinese cooking wine (*hua diao*) *300 ml (10 fl oz / 1¹/₄ cups)*

Tomato sauce *100 ml (3¹/₂ fl oz)*

Mushroom flavoured sauce *2 tsp*

Ginger *2 slices*

Nutmeg *1*

Bay leaf *1*

Cinnamon stick *1*

Spring onion (scallion) *¹/₂*

Rock sugar *100 g (3¹/₂ oz)*

1. Using a kitchen torch, lightly torch pork belly to remove any hair on skin. Alternatively, burn it using an open flame on the stove top. Cut pork belly into cubes, then marinate with light soy sauce.

2. Heat oil for deep-frying and deep-fry pork belly for 3 minutes until lightly browned. Remove pork belly and rinse with cold water to remove the oil.

3. Put pork belly, chicken stock, ingredients for seasoning and aromatics in a pot. Simmer over low heat for 1¹/₂ hours until meat is tender and stock has thickened slightly. Alternatively, use a pressure cooker to reduce the cooking time to 30 minutes.

4. Skim off and discard the layer of fat from the stock, then strain and reheat stock. Stir in corn flour mixture to thicken stock.

5. Place pickled bamboo shoot on a serving plate. Top with pork belly and serve.

NOTE Pickled bamboo shoot with chilli is available in jars from the supermarket. Rinse with hot water to remove the spiciness, if desired.

Braised Pork Trotters & Peanuts Serves 4

BRAISED PORK TROTTERS

Pork trotters *500 g (1 lb 1¹/₂ oz)*

Light soy sauce *2 Tbsp*

Cooking oil *for deep-frying*

Ginger *2 slices*

Spring onion (scallion) *1*

Garlic *1 clove*

Celery *20 g (²/₃ oz)*

Carrot *20 g (²/₃ oz)*

Big white onion *20 g (²/₃ oz)*

Bay leaf *1*

Star anise *1*

Chinese red dates *5*

Chinese wolfberries *2 tsp*

Water *2 litres (64 fl oz / 8 cups)*

Mushroom flavoured sauce *2 Tbsp*

Rock sugar *50 g (1²/₃ oz)*

Oyster sauce *1 Tbsp*

Dark soy sauce *a dash*

Red yeast rice (*hong qu mi*) *¹/₂ Tbsp*

Corn flour (cornstarch) *¹/₂ tsp, mixed with 2 tsp water*

BRAISED PEANUTS

Peanuts *100 g (3¹/₂ oz)*

Chicken stock (page 159) *250 ml (8 fl oz / 1 cup)*

Bay leaf *1*

Cinnamon stick *1*

Rock sugar *10 g (¹/₃ oz)*

Oyster sauce *2 tsp*

Mushroom flavoured sauce *2 tsp*

Honey *2 tsp*

Chinese cooking wine (*hua diao*) *1 Tbsp*

1. Prepare pork trotters. Using a kitchen torch, lightly torch trotters to remove any hair on skin. Alternatively, burn it using an open flame on the stove top. Chop trotters into smaller pieces, then rub light soy sauce all over them.

2. Heat cooking oil and deep-fry trotters for 3 minutes until brown. Remove and rinse with water to remove all traces of oil. Set aside.

3. Put remaining ingredients for trotters, except corn flour, into a pot and simmer over low heat for 1 hour until meat is tender and stock has thickened slightly. Alternatively, use a pressure cooker to reduce the cooking time to 20 minutes.

4. Meanwhile, prepare braised peanuts. Put all ingredients into a pot and cook over low heat for about 30 minutes until peanuts are soft. Remove peanuts and discard other ingredients. Place on a serving dish.

5. Remove trotters from stock and put into prepared serving dish with peanuts.

6. Skim off and discard the layer of fat from stock, then strain and reheat stock. Stir in corn flour mixture to thicken stock. Pour stock over pork trotters and serve.

My Grandmother's Steamed Minced Pork Petites with Salted Egg Yolk Serves 4

Minced pork shoulder *400 g (14¹/₃ oz)*

Minced pork fat *1 Tbsp*

Coriander (cilantro) stems *30 g (1 oz), minced*

Water chestnuts *3, peeled and minced*

Salt *1 tsp*

Sugar *1 tsp*

Light soy sauce *2 tsp*

Egg white *1*

Ground white pepper *a pinch*

Sesame oil *a dash*

Corn oil *as needed*

Salted egg yolks *4*

Homemade soy sauce (page 160) *200 ml (7 fl oz)*

Spring onion (scallion) *1, minced*

1. Combine all ingredients, except corn oil, salted egg yolks, homemade soy sauce and spring onions, in a mixing bowl and mix well.

2. Apply some corn oil on the inside of 4 small stainless steel cups, Chinese teacups or small rice bowls. Put a salted egg yolk inside each cup/bowl, then spoon pork mixture in to fill cups/bowls.

3. Place cups/bowls in a steamer and steam for 1 hour or until minced pork is cooked.

4. Turn cups/bowls over and the meat will slide out. Serve with homemade soy sauce. Garnish with spring onion.

NOTE Adding pork fat makes these steamed minced pork petites flavourful and juicy. You can omit the pork fat for a healthier option, but the resulting dish will not be as moist and tasty.

Sliced Pork with Garlic Vinaigrette Sauce Serves 4

Thinly sliced pork belly *200 g (7 oz)*

GARLIC VINAIGRETTE

Garlic *1 head, peeled and minced*

Japanese sweet barbecue sauce *3 Tbsp*

Dark soy sauce *1/2 Tbsp*

Chilli oil *1 Tbsp*

Sesame oil *1/2 Tbsp*

Honey *2 Tbsp*

Red bean curd *1 Tbsp*

Black vinegar *2 Tbsp*

Corn oil *2 Tbsp*

GARNISH

Coriander leaves (cilantro) *1 sprig*

Red chilli *1, seeded, then cut into thin strips*

1. Bring a pot of water to the boil. Add pork belly and poach very briefly to cook pork lightly. Drain well and arrange on a serving plate.

2. Put ingredients for garlic vinaigrette into a bowl and mix well. Pour over pork belly and garnish with coriander leaves and shredded red chilli.

NOTE You can use the thinly sliced pork belly for Japanese shabu shabu for this dish. It is available in the Japanese food section of some supermarkets.

Steamed Minced Pork with Sichuan Pickled Cabbage Serves 4

Minced pork belly *350 g (12 oz)*

Sichuan pickled cabbage *80 g (3 oz), sliced*

Ginger *10 g (¹/₃ oz), peeled and shredded*

Cooking oil *2 Tbsp*

Homemade soy sauce (page 160) *2 Tbsp*

Chives *a small bunch, chopped*

SEASONING (COMBINED)

Chicken stock (page 159) or water *1 Tbsp*

Oyster sauce *1 Tbsp*

Mushroom flavoured sauce *¹/₂ Tbsp*

Dark soy sauce *a dash*

Chinese cooking wine (*hua diao*) *1 Tbsp*

Sesame oil *¹/₂ Tbsp*

Sugar *¹/₄ Tbsp*

Egg white *1*

Corn flour (cornstarch) *¹/₂ Tbsp*

1. Mix minced pork with ingredients for seasoning and set aside for 10 minutes.

2. Put pork in a shallow steaming dish and press it down lightly to form a thin disc, so the pork will cook quickly and easily.

3. Top pork with pickled cabbage and ginger. Place in a steamer and steam for 15 minutes until pork is cooked. Remove and set aside.

4. Heat oil in a wok and pour over pork. Do the same with homemade soy sauce. Garnish with chives and serve immediately.

NOTE To reduce the saltiness of the pickled cabbage, soak in hot water for 2 minutes before using.

Crispy Pork Ribs Coated with Five-Spice Powder Serves 4

Pork ribs *400 g (14¹/₃ oz), cut into bite-size pieces*

Water *1.5 litres (48 fl oz / 6 cups)*

Ginger *3 slices*

Spring onion (scallion) *¹/₂*

Dried chillies *5*

Red chillies *2*

Star anise *1*

Bay leaf *1*

Oyster sauce *2 tsp*

Dark soy sauce *¹/₈ tsp*

Chinese cooking wine (*hua diao*) *3 tsp*

Sugar *1 tsp*

Cooking oil *for deep-frying*

Corn flour (cornstarch) *200 g (7 oz)*

FIVE-SPICE SEASONING (COMBINED)

Chicken stock (page 159) *100 ml (3¹/₂ fl oz)*

Salt *¹/₂ tsp*

Honey *¹/₂ tsp*

Sweet mirin *¹/₂ tsp*

Sake *¹/₂ tsp*

Lemon juice *1 tsp*

Minced garlic *1 tsp*

Minced ginger *1 tsp*

Minced torch ginger bud *1 tsp*

Five-spice powder *¹/₂ tsp, mixed with 1 Tbsp Chinese cooking wine (hua diao)*

1. Bring a pot of water to the boil and poach pork ribs to remove any surface scum. Drain.

2. Put pork ribs in a pot and add water and all remaining ingredients, except cooking oil and corn flour. Simmer over low heat for 1¹/₂ hours or until pork ribs are tender. Remove ribs and discard contents of pot.

3. Heat cooking oil for deep-frying. Coat ribs with corn flour and deep-fry until brown and crisp. Remove and drain well.

4. Heat ¹/₂ Tbsp oil in a wok. Add pork ribs and five-spice seasoning and toss well. Dish out and serve.

Slow-poached Beef in Sweet Soy Sauce Serves 4

Cooking oil *1 Tbsp*

White hon shimeji mushrooms *80 g (3 oz), base trimmed*

Spring onion (scallion) *1, cut into short lengths*

Chicken stock (page 159) *200 ml (7 fl oz)*

Thinly sliced beef *200 g (7 oz)*

Chinese wolfberries *1 tsp, soaked in water for 10 minutes*

SEASONING (COMBINED)

Mushroom flavoured sauce *1 Tbsp*

Light soy sauce *1 Tbsp*

Sweet mirin *1 Tbsp*

Sake *1/2 Tbsp*

Honey *1/2 Tbsp*

Vodka *1/2 Tbsp*

Lemon juice *1/2 Tbsp*

1. Heat oil in a wok and sear mushrooms lightly. Add spring onion and stir-fry until fragrant.

2. Add chicken stock and ingredients for seasoning. Bring to the boil, then lower heat to medium. Add beef and cook lightly.

3. Dish out and garnish with Chinese wolfberries.

NOTE You can use the thinly sliced beef for Japanese shabu shabu for this dish. It is available in the Japanese food section of some supermarkets.

Pan-seared Beef Rolls with Black Pepper Sauce Serves 4

Beef *250 g (9 oz), thinly sliced*

Enoki mushrooms *300 g (11 oz), base trimmed*

Corn flour (cornstarch) *1 tsp, mixed with 3 tsp water*

Cooking oil *2 Tbsp*

Coriander leaves (cilantro) *1 sprig*

BLACK PEPPER SAUCE

Butter *2 Tbsp*

Garlic *15 g (¹/₂ oz), peeled and minced*

Red chillies *15 g (¹/₂ oz), minced*

Mint leaves *10 g (¹/₃ oz), minced*

Water *200 ml (7 fl oz)*

Black peppercorns *15 g (¹/₂ oz), crushed*

Maggi seasoning *2 Tbsp*

Icing (confectioner's) sugar *4 Tbsp*

Worcestershire sauce *2 tsp*

Tomato sauce *4 Tbsp*

Dark soy sauce *10 Tbsp*

Plain (all purpose) flour *1 Tbsp*

1. Start by preparing black pepper sauce. (Alternatively, bottled black pepper sauce is available from the supermarkets.) Heat butter in a wok and add minced garlic. Stir-fry lightly, then add chillies, mint leaves and water. Bring to the boil and add remaining ingredients. Mix well. Remove from heat and set aside.

2. Lay a slice of beef flat on a clean work surface. Place some mushrooms on one edge of beef and roll up. Seal roll using corn flour mixture. Repeat until ingredients are used up.

3. Heat cooking oil in a pan and sear beef rolls. Cook to your preferred level of doneness.

4. Reheat black pepper sauce and spoon over beef rolls. Garnish with coriander leaves and serve.

NOTE You can use the thinly sliced beef for Japanese shabu shabu for this dish. It is available in the Japanese food section of some supermarkets.

Slow-stewed Beef Cubes with Radish Serves 4

Beef knuckle *400 g (14¹/₃ oz), cut into cubes*

Garlic *5 cloves, peeled*

Chinese red dates *5*

Ginger *10 slices*

Coriander leaves (cilantro) *2 sprigs*

Cinnamon stick *1*

Star anise *2*

White radish *200 g (7 oz), peeled and cut into cubes*

Chicken stock (page 159) *2 litres (64 fl oz / 8 cups)*

Yellow bean sauce *2 Tbsp*

Oyster sauce *3 Tbsp*

Rock sugar *30 g (1 oz)*

Dark soy sauce *1 Tbsp*

Chinese cooking wine (*hua diao*) *1 Tbsp*

Cooking oil *2 Tbsp*

Corn flour (cornstarch) *¹/₂ tsp, mixed with 2 tsp water*

Chives *a small bunch, chopped*

1. Bring a pot of water to the boil and poach beef knuckle to remove any surface scum. Drain.

2. Place beef in a pot with all remaining ingredients except corn flour and chives. Simmer over low heat for 30 minutes, then remove white radish which should be cooked by now.

3. Continue to simmer beef for another 30 minutes until beef is completely soft and tender. Remove beef and strain stock.

4. Heat oil in a wok and add radish and beef. Stir-fry until fragrant. Add stock and bring to the boil. Stir in corn flour to thicken stock.

5. Dish out and garnish with chives. Serve hot.

Poached Boneless Chicken with Warm Ginger Sauce

Serves 4

Chicken *1, about 1.5 kg (3 lb 4¹/₂ oz)*

Ginger *2 slices*

Spring onion (scallion) *1*

Salt *1 tsp*

Sugar *1 tsp*

GINGER SAUCE

Corn oil *1 Tbsp*

Ginger *100 g (3¹/₂ oz), peeled and minced*

Spring onions (scallions) *100 g (3¹/₂ oz), white part only, minced*

Sesame oil *¹/₂ Tbsp*

Chinese cooking wine (*hua diao*) *1 tsp*

Salt *¹/₂ tsp*

Sugar *¹/₂ tsp*

1. Rinse chicken and drain well.

2. Bring a large pot of water to the boil over medium heat and add ginger, spring onion, salt and sugar. Add chicken and cook for 10 minutes over medium heat. Reduce heat to low and let chicken cook gently for 10 minutes.

3. Using a pair of cooking chopsticks or tongs, lift chicken up and let the water drain from the chicken back into the pot. Return chicken to pot and continue to cook over low heat for another 15 minutes.

4. Remove chicken and drain, then soak in cold water for 20 minutes until chicken is cooled. Debone chicken and cut into bite-size pieces. Place on a serving plate.

5. Prepare ginger sauce. Heat 1 tsp corn oil in a wok over low heat. Add ginger and spring onions and stir-fry until heated through. Add remaining ingredients and mix well.

6. Ladle warm ginger sauce over chicken and serve.

NOTE Cooked this way, the chicken is moist and succulent. You can also try using Sakura chicken, a chicken farmed using Japanese farming technology.

My Grandmother's Steamed Chicken with Fermented Bean Curd <small>Serves 4</small>

Boneless chicken *350 g (12 oz), diced*

Chinese sausages *50 g (1²/₃ oz), sliced*

Ginger *10 g (¹/₃ oz), peeled and shredded*

White hon shimeji mushrooms *80 g (3 oz), base trimmed*

Fermented bean curd (*fu ru*) *2 cubes, mashed*

Cooking oil *2 Tbsp*

Homemade soy sauce (page 160) *2 Tbsp*

Chives *a small bunch, chopped*

SEASONING (COMBINED)
Oyster sauce *1 Tbsp*

Mushroom flavoured sauce *¹/₂ Tbsp*

Dark soy sauce *a dash*

Sesame oil *¹/₂ Tbsp*

Chinese cooking wine (*hua diao*) *1 Tbsp*

Egg white *1*

Sugar *¹/₄ Tbsp*

Corn flour (cornstarch) *¹/₂ Tbsp*

1. Marinate chicken with ingredients for seasoning and set aside for 10 minutes.

2. Put chicken into a steaming plate and top with sausages, ginger, mushrooms and fermented bean curd. Steam for 15 minutes until chicken is cooked. Remove and set aside.

3. Heat oil in a wok and pour over chicken. Do the same with homemade soy sauce. Garnish with chives and serve immediately.

Vegetables
& Bean Curd

Steamed Angled Luffa with Stir-fried Dried Prawns
   & Minced Pork 98

Mustard Greens Stir-fried with Dried Scallops 100

Lily Bulb, Asparagus, Black Fungus & Gingko Nut Stir-fry 102

Aubergine & Minced Pork Stir-fry 104

Bamboo Shoot with Preserved Vegetables 106

Poached Chinese Cabbage with Salted Egg Yolk, Century Egg
   & Dried Scallops 108

Broad Beans Stir-fried with Dried Prawns & Garlic 110

Long Beans Stir-fried with Minced Chicken & XO Sauce 112

Bean Curd Stir-fry 114

Bean Curd Topped with Prawn Paste & Black Bean Sauce 116

Spicy Mapo Bean Curd with Minced Pork & Minced Fish 118

Steamed Angled Luffa with Stir-fried Dried Prawns & Minced Pork Serves 4

Angled luffa *800 g (1³/₄ lb)*

Dried prawns (shrimps) *2 Tbsp, soaked in water for 10 minutes*

Cooking oil *2 Tbsp*

Minced garlic *1 tsp*

Minced ginger *1 tsp*

Red chilli *1, seeded and minced*

Preserved turnip *1 tsp*

Minced pork shoulder *200 g (7 oz)*

Corn flour (cornstarch) *¹/₂ tsp, mixed with 2 tsp water*

Chives *a small bunch, chopped*

CRISPY SOY BEAN CRUMB

Soy bean crumb *1 piece*

Cooking oil *1 Tbsp*

Minced ginger *¹/₂ tsp*

Minced garlic *¹/₂ tsp*

SEASONING (COMBINED)

Chicken stock (page 159) or water *3 Tbsp*

Yellow bean sauce *¹/₂ tsp*

Oyster sauce *1 tsp*

Mushroom flavoured sauce *¹/₂ tsp*

Sugar *¹/₂ tsp*

1. Start by preparing crispy soy bean crumb. Steam soy bean crumb for 10 minutes, then mince until fine. Heat oil in a wok and add ginger and garlic. Stir-fry until fragrant, then add soy bean crumb and stir-fry until crisp. Set aside until needed.

2. Peel angled luffa and cut into 2.5-cm (1-in) thick rounds. Use a melon baller to scoop out the centre. Sprinkle a little salt over angled luffa and steam for 5 minutes.

3. Drain dried prawns and mince until fine. Heat oil in a wok and stir-fry dried prawns until fragrant, crisp and brown. Add garlic, ginger, chilli and preserved turnip, and stir-fry until fragrant.

4. Add minced pork and mix well. Add ingredients for seasoning, then stir in corn flour mixture to thicken sauce. Fill angled luffa with pork mixture and steam for 2 minutes.

5. Garnish with chives and crispy soy bean crumb. Serve hot.

NOTE Be careful not to overcook the soy bean crumb or it might become bitter. It is ready once it turns crisp.

Mustard Greens Stir-fried with Dried Scallops Serves 4

Mustard greens *800 g (1³/₄ lb)*

Cooking oil *2 Tbsp*

Chicken stock (page 159) *200 ml (7 fl oz)*

Oyster sauce *2 tsp*

Dark soy sauce *a dash*

Chinese cooking wine (*hua diao*) *a dash*

Sugar *¹/₄ tsp*

Steamed dried scallops (page 159) *12 pieces*

Corn flour (cornstarch) *¹/₂ tsp, mixed with 2 tsp water*

1. Cut mustard greens into bite-size pieces. Bring a pot of water to the boil and blanch mustard greens for about 4 minutes until soft.

2. Heat oil in a wok and add chicken stock, oyster sauce, dark soy sauce, Chinese cooking wine and sugar. Bring to the boil and add dried scallops.

3. Stir in corn flour to thicken stock, then pour over mustard greens. Serve hot.

NOTE To keep the mustard greens from turning yellow when blanching, add 1 tsp alkaline water to the pot. This will not only help the mustard greens retain their attractive green colour, it will also help in giving them a softer texture. After blanching, drain and plunge the mustard greens immediately into iced water to stop the cooking process.

Lily Bulb, Asparagus, Black Fungus & Gingko Nut Stir-fry Serves 4

Black fungus *10 g (¹/₃ oz), soaked in water for 1 hour*

Green asparagus *300 g (11 oz), cut into pieces*

Ready-prepared or canned gingko nuts *50 g (1²/₃ oz)*

Fresh lily bulbs *100 g (3¹/₂ oz)*

Cooking oil *1 Tbsp*

Corn flour (corn starch) *¹/₂ tsp, mixed with 2 tsp water*

Chinese wolfberries *2 tsp, soaked in water for 10 minutes*

GINGER JUICE

Ginger *50 g (1²/₃ oz), peeled and chopped*

Water *100 ml (3¹/₂ fl oz)*

SEASONING

Chicken stock (page 159) or water *4 Tbsp*

Salt *¹/₂ tsp*

Sugar *¹/₂ tsp*

Sesame oil *a dash*

Chinese cooking wine (*hua diao*) *a dash*

1. Prepare ginger juice. Put ginger and water in a blender and process. Strain. Measure out ¹/₂ tsp and mix with other ingredients for seasoning. Set aside. (It is difficult to prepare a smaller amount of ginger juice using the blender, so use the remaining ginger juice to flavour other dishes.)

2. Put soaked black fungus in a bowl and cover with hot water. Steam for 30 minutes until soft.

3. Bring a pot of water to the boil and poach asparagus, gingko nuts and lily bulbs for about 20 seconds. Drain and set aside.

4. Heat oil in a wok and add black fungus, asparagus, gingko nuts and lily bulbs and stir-fry until fragrant. Add ingredients for seasoning, then stir in corn flour mixture to thicken sauce.

5. Dish out and garnish with wolfberries. Serve hot.

Aubergine & Minced Pork Stir-fry Serves 4

Cooking oil *for deep-frying*

Aubergines (brinjals/eggplants) *500 g (1 lb 1¹/₂ oz), cut into 5-cm (2-in) lengths*

Minced pork shoulder *150 g (5¹/₃ oz)*

Fresh shiitake mushrooms *100 g (3¹/₂ oz), thinly sliced*

Spring onion (scallion) *1, chopped*

Red chilli *1, sliced*

Minced garlic *¹/₂ tsp*

Minced ginger *¹/₂ tsp*

Chicken stock (page 159) *200 ml (7 fl oz)*

Corn flour (cornstarch) *¹/₂ tsp, mixed with 2 tsp water*

SEASONING (COMBINED)

Oyster sauce *1 tsp*

Hot bean sauce *3 tsp*

Tomato sauce *3 tsp*

Dark soy sauce *a dash*

Chinese cooking wine (*hua diao*) *a dash*

Sesame oil *¹/₂ tsp*

Sugar *¹/₂ tsp*

1. Heat oil for deep-frying and deep-fry aubergines briefly until brown. Drain and set aside.

2. Bring a pot of water to the boil. Place minced pork and mushrooms in a strainer and dip into hot water for 10 seconds. Drain and set aside.

3. Heat 1 Tbsp oil in a wok. Add spring onions, chillies, garlic and ginger and stir-fry until fragrant. Add aubergines, minced pork, mushrooms, chicken stock and ingredients for seasoning. Simmer for 2 minutes until stock is reduced.

4. Stir in corn flour mixture to thicken sauce. Dish out and serve hot.

Bamboo Shoot with Preserved Vegetables Serves 4

Fresh or canned bamboo shoot
  400 g (14¹/₃ oz)

Cooking oil *1 Tbsp*

Minced garlic *¹/₂ tsp*

Minced ginger *¹/₂ tsp*

Preserved vegetable (*xue cai*)
  200 g (7 oz)

Corn flour (cornstarch) *¹/₂ tsp, mixed
  with 2 tsp water*

Chives *a small bunch, chopped*

SEASONING (COMBINED)

Chicken stock (page 159) *80 ml
  (2¹/₂ fl oz / ¹/₃ cup)*

Oyster sauce *2 tsp*

Sugar *¹/₂ tsp*

Sesame oil *a dash*

Chinese cooking wine (*hua diao*)
  a dash

1. Bring a pot of water to the boil. If using canned bamboo shoot, add to pot and boil for 10 minutes. Remove and drain. For fresh bamboo shoot, add to pot and boil for 30 minutes. Discard water and bring a new pot of water to the boil. Add boiled fresh bamboo shoot and cook for another 10 minutes.

2. Cut bamboo shoot into cubes.

3. Heat oil in a wok and add minced garlic and ginger. Stir-fry until fragrant, then add bamboo shoot and preserved vegetable. Stir-fry until fragrant, then add ingredients for seasoning and thicken with corn flour mixture.

4. Dish out and garnish with chives. Serve hot.

Poached Chinese Cabbage with Salted Egg Yolk, Century Egg & Dried Scallops Serves 4

Cooking oil *for deep-frying*

Chinese cabbage (stems only)
600 g (1 lb 5¹/₃ oz), cut into 5-cm (2-in) squares

Salted egg yolks *3, cut into small cubes*

Century egg *1, peeled and cut into small cubes*

Steamed dried scallops (page 159) *4 pieces*

Corn flour (cornstarch) *¹/₂ tsp, mixed with 2 tsp water*

Chives *a small bunch, chopped*

SEASONING (COMBINED)
Chicken stock (page 159) *150 ml (5 fl oz / 10 Tbsp)*

Salt *¹/₂ tsp*

Sugar *¹/₄ tsp*

Ground white pepper *a dash*

Chinese cooking wine (*hua diao*) *a dash*

1. Heat oil for deep-frying and briefly deep-fry Chinese cabbage until slightly brown. Remove.

2. Bring a pot of water to the boil and add cabbage. Boil for about 20 minutes or until cabbage is done to your preference. Drain and place on a serving plate.

3. Meanwhile, place salted egg yolks on a steaming plate and steam for about 10 minutes until cooked.

4. Heat 1 Tbsp oil in a wok and add ingredients for seasoning. Bring to the boil, then add salted egg yolks, century egg and dried scallops. Stir in corn flour to thicken sauce, then pour over cabbage. Garnish with chives and serve.

Broad Beans Stir-fried with Dried Prawns & Garlic Serves 4

Cooking oil *for deep-frying*

Broad beans *400 g (14$^1/_3$ oz),
cut into short lengths*

Dried prawns (shrimps) *3 Tbsp,
soaked in water for 10 minutes*

Crispy whole garlic (page 161)
1 Tbsp

Red chilli *1, sliced*

Fermented black beans *$^1/_2$ Tbsp,
rinsed*

Corn flour (cornstarch) *$^1/_2$ tsp,
mixed with 2 tsp water*

White sesame seeds *1 tsp, toasted*

SEASONING (COMBINED)

Chicken stock (page 159) or water
4 Tbsp

Oyster sauce *2 tsp*

Dark soy sauce *a dash*

White miso paste *1 tsp*

Yellow bean sauce *1 tsp*

Sesame oil *a dash*

Chinese cooking wine (*hua diao*)
a dash

Sugar *$^1/_8$ tsp*

1. Heat oil for deep-frying and deep-fry broad beans for 1 minute until broad beans have shrunk. Drain and set aside.

2. Heat 1 Tbsp oil in a wok and sauté dried prawns until crisp and fragrant, then add crispy whole garlic, chilli and fermented black beans. Stir-fry briefly.

3. Add ingredients for seasoning and stir-fry until fragrant. Stir in corn flour mixture to thicken sauce.

4. Dish out and garnish with sesame seeds. Serve hot.

Long Beans Stir-fried with Minced Chicken & XO Sauce Serves 4

Cooking oil *for deep-frying*

Long beans *400 g (14¹/₃ oz),*
  cut into 4-cm (1¹/₂-in) lengths

Minced chicken *100 g (3¹/₂ oz)*

Fresh shiitake mushrooms *3,*
  minced

Minced garlic *1 tsp*

Minced ginger *1 tsp*

Fermented black beans *1 tsp, rinsed*

Red chilli *1, seeded and minced*

Corn flour (cornstarch) *¹/₂ tsp, mixed*
  with 2 tsp water

SEASONING (COMBINED)

Chicken stock (page 159) or water
  80 ml (2¹/₂ fl oz / ¹/₃ cup)

XO sauce *2 Tbsp*

Oyster sauce *¹/₂ tsp*

Sugar *¹/₈ tsp*

Sesame oil *a dash*

Chinese cooking wine (*hua diao*)
  a dash

1. Heat oil for deep-frying and deep-fry long beans for 1 minute until long beans have shrunk. Drain and set aside.

2. Bring a pot of water to the boil. Put minced pork and mushrooms into a strainer and dip into hot water for 10 seconds. Drain and set aside.

3. Heat 1 Tbsp oil in a wok and add garlic, ginger, fermented black beans and chilli. Stir-fry until fragrant.

4. Add long beans, minced chicken and mushrooms, together with ingredients for seasoning. Stir-fry until fragrant, then stir in corn flour mixture to thicken sauce.

5. Dish out and serve hot.

Bean Curd Stir-fry Serves 4

Firm bean curd *300 g (11 oz)*

Cooking oil *for deep-frying*

Minced garlic *$1/2$ tsp*

Minced ginger *$1/2$ tsp*

White hon shimeji mushrooms *50 g (1$2/3$ oz) , blanched with hot water*

Spring onion (scallion) *1, chopped*

Red chilli *1, sliced*

Crispy whole garlic (page 161) *1 Tbsp*

Corn flour (cornstarch) *$1/2$ tsp, mixed with 2 tsp water*

Basil leaves *a handful*

Coriander (cilantro) leaves *1 sprig*

SEASONING (COMBINED)

Chicken stock (page 159) *125 ml (4 fl oz / $1/2$ cup)*

Hot bean paste *2 tsp*

Tomato sauce *2 tsp*

Chilli sauce *1 tsp*

Yellow bean sauce *$1/2$ tsp*

Sugar *$1/8$ tsp*

Sesame oil *a dash*

Dark soy sauce *a dash*

Chinese cooking wine (*hua diao*) *a dash*

1. Cut firm bean curd into thin slices, then cut into triangles.

2. Heat oil for deep-frying and deep-fry bean curd until crisp and brown. Drain well.

3. Heat 1 Tbsp oil in a wok and add minced garlic and ginger and stir-fry until fragrant. Add bean curd, mushrooms, spring onion, chilli, crispy whole garlic and ingredients for seasoning. Stir-fry briefly.

4. Add corn flour mixture to thicken sauce, then add basil leaves. Dish out and garnish with coriander leaves. Serve.

NOTE As a variation to this recipe, substitute firm bean curd with egg bean curd.

Bean Curd Topped with Prawn Paste & Black Bean Sauce Serves 4

Prawns (shrimps) *200 g (7 oz)*

Minced coriander (cilantro) stems *1/2 Tbsp*

Water chestnuts *3, peeled and chopped*

Silken bean curd *2 tubes, each 250 g (9 oz), cut to get 12 rounds*

Corn flour (cornstarch) *1/2 tsp, mixed with 2 tsp water*

Chives *a small bunch, chopped*

SEASONING

Salt *1/2 tsp*

Sugar *1 tsp*

Sesame oil *1/2 tsp*

Egg white *1*

Corn flour (cornstarch) *1/2 tsp*

Ground white pepper *1/2 tsp*

SAUCE

Cooking oil *1 Tbsp*

Fermented black beans *3 tsp, rinsed and minced*

Chicken stock (page 159) *150 ml (5 fl oz / 10 Tbsp)*

Oyster sauce *1 tsp*

Dark soy sauce *a dash*

Yellow bean sauce *1/2 tsp*

Sugar *1/2 tsp*

Sesame oil *a dash*

Chinese cooking wine (*hua diao*) *a dash*

1. Peel and devein prawns. Rinse, then chop using the spine of a cleaver until mixture is pasty. Mix prawn paste with coriander stems, water chestnuts and ingredients for seasoning. Set aside.

2. Using a melon baller, scoop a bit off the top of each round of bean curd. Place bean curd on a steaming plate.

3. Shape prawn mixture into balls and place on bean curd rounds. Steam for 5 minutes until cooked.

4. Meanwhile, prepare sauce. Heat oil in a wok over medium heat. Add minced fermented black beans and stir-fry until fragrant. Add remaining ingredients until heated through.

5. Stir in corn flour mixture to thicken sauce, then pour over bean curd. Garnish with chives and serve.

Spicy Mapo Bean Curd with Minced Pork & Minced Fish Serves 4

Silken bean curd *3 tubes, each 250 g (9 oz), diced*

Minced pork shoulder *100 g (3¹/₂ oz)*

Fresh shiitake mushrooms *5, minced*

White fish fillet (any kind) *100 g (3¹/₂ oz), minced*

Cooking oil *1 Tbsp*

Minced ginger *¹/₂ tsp*

Minced shallot *¹/₂ tsp*

Minced garlic *¹/₂ tsp*

Spring onion (scallion) *1, chopped*

Red chilli *1, sliced*

Chicken stock (page 159) *200 ml (7 fl oz)*

Corn flour (cornstarch) *¹/₂ tsp, mixed with 2 tsp water*

SEASONING (COMBINED)

Hot bean paste *2 tsp*

Tomato sauce *3 tsp*

Chilli sauce *3 tsp*

Oyster sauce *1 tsp*

Sugar *1 tsp*

OPTIONAL

Sichuan pepper oil (page 161) *2 tsp*

Sichuan pepper (page 161) *¹/₈ tsp*

1. Bring a pot of water to the boil. Put bean curd into a strainer and dip briefly into hot water. Drain and set aside.

2. Return water to the boil and repeat to cook minced pork, mushrooms and fish. Drain and set aside.

3. Heat oil in a wok and add minced ginger, shallot and garlic. Stir-fry until fragrant, then add spring onion, chilli, bean curd, pork, mushrooms, fish and ingredients for seasoning. Stir-fry to mix.

4. Add chicken stock and bring to the boil. Stir in corn flour mixture to thicken sauce.

5. Dish out and drizzle with Sichuan pepper oil and Sichuan pepper, if desired. Serve hot.

Rice &
Noodles

Radish Cake with Seafood & XO Sauce 122

Steamed Glutinous Rice with Pork Ribs 124

Seafood Fried Rice 126

Steamed Fragrant Rice with Minced Pork,
    Chinese Sausages & Mushrooms 128

Steamed Glutinous Rice with Crab 130

Malaysian-style Noodles with XO Sauce 132

Wok-fried Vermicelli with Crab 134

Fish Head Noodles 136

My Grandmother's Handmade Noodles 138

Radish Cake with Seafood & XO Sauce Serves 4

Prawns (shrimps) *8, medium, peeled*

Scallops *4*

Crabmeat *100 g (3^1/$_2$ oz)*

Cooking oil *1 Tbsp*

Bean sprouts *100 g (3^1/$_2$ oz)*

Yellow chives *100 g (3^1/$_2$ oz)*

Spring onions (scallions) *100 g (3^1/$_2$ oz)*

Eggs *2, beaten*

RADISH CAKE

Cooking oil *2 Tbsp*

Dried prawns (shrimps) *^{1}/$_2$ Tbsp, soaked in water for 10 minutes, then minced*

Chinese sausage *^{1}/$_2$, minced*

Fresh shiitake mushrooms *2, minced*

Water *500 ml (16 fl oz / 2 cups)*

Glutinous rice flour *75 g (2^1/$_2$ oz)*

Potato flour *20 g (^{2}/$_3$ oz)*

Corn flour (cornstarch) *20 g (^{2}/$_3$ oz)*

White radish *100 g (3^1/$_2$ oz), peeled and shredded*

Sugar *^{1}/$_2$ Tbsp*

Salt *^{1}/$_2$ tsp*

SEASONING (COMBINED)

Chicken stock (page 159) or water *4 Tbsp*

XO sauce *1 Tbsp*

Oyster sauce *^{1}/$_2$ tsp*

Sugar *^{1}/$_8$ tsp*

Dark soy sauce *a dash*

Sesame oil *a dash*

Chinese cooking wine (*hua diao*) *a dash*

1. Prepare radish cake. Heat 1 Tbsp oil in a wok and stir-fry dried prawns, Chinese sausage and mushrooms until fragrant and dried prawns and sausages are crisp. Set aside.

2. Mix half the water with glutinous rice flour, potato flour and corn flour. Set aside. Mix remaining water with radish, dried prawns, sausages, mushrooms sugar and salt. Combine both mixtures and pour into a 21-cm (8-in) square baking tray. Place in a steamer and steam for 35 minutes. Leave to cool before cutting into 3-cm (1-in) cubes.

3. Heat remaining oil in a wok and sear radish cake until brown and lightly crisp. Set aside.

4. Bring a pot of water to the boil. Place prawns, scallops and crabmeat into a strainer and dip briefly into hot water to cook lightly. Drain and set aside.

5. Heat oil in a wok and add bean sprouts, yellow chives and spring onions. Stir-fry briefly, then add eggs and cook until just beginning to set.

6. Add radish cake and ingredients for seasoning. Fry until fragrant and egg is cooked. Dish out and serve hot.

Steamed Glutinous Rice with Pork Ribs Serves 4

Pork ribs *400 g (14¹/₃ oz)*

Glutinous rice *200 g (7 oz)*

Chives *a small bunch, chopped*

MARINADE (COMBINED)

Fermented bean curd (*fu ru*)
  2 cubes

Plum oil *4 tsp*

Fermented black beans *¹/₂ tsp*

Yellow bean sauce *¹/₂ tsp*

Sugar *1 tsp*

Sesame oil *a dash*

Egg *1*

Dark soy sauce *a dash*

Minced coriander (cilantro) stems
  3 tsp

Minced garlic *3 tsp*

Chinese cooking wine (*hua diao*)
  a dash

1. Start preparations a day ahead.

2. Place pork ribs in a bowl and add ingredients for marinade. Mix well, cover and refrigerate overnight.

3. Soak glutinous rice in water overnight.

4. The following day, drain rice, then place into an oiled steaming tray and steam for 45 minutes until rice is soft and sticky.

5. Mix steamed glutinous rice with pork ribs and steam for another 10 minutes until pork ribs are cooked.

6. Dish out and garnish with chives. Serve hot.

NOTE If the glutinous rice becomes thick and gluey after steaming, place it into hot water for 3 minutes, then drain. It will become less lumpy.

Seafood Fried Rice Serves 4

Prawns (shrimps) *250 g (9 oz), peeled and diced*

Scallops *150 g (5¹/₃ oz), diced*

Crabmeat *100 g (3¹/₂ oz)*

Carrot *¹/₃ medium, peeled and diced*

Thai asparagus *10 stalks, diced*

Cooking oil *for deep-frying*

Eggs *3, beaten*

Cooked long-grain rice *2 Chinese rice bowls*

Steamed dried scallops (page 159) *4 pieces*

SEASONING (COMBINED)

Salt *³/₄ tsp*

Sugar *¹/₂ tsp*

Ground white pepper *a pinch*

Chives *a small bunch, chopped*

1. Bring a pot of water to the boil and briefly blanch prawns, scallops, crabmeat, carrot and asparagus to cook lightly. Drain and set aside.

2. Heat 1 Tbsp oil in a wok and add eggs. When eggs are starting to set, scramble them, then add blanched seafood and cooked rice and stir-fry until fragrant.

3. Add ingredients for seasoning and stir-fry until rice is fragrant once again.

4. Drain steamed dried scallops and separate into shreds. Heat oil for deep-frying and deep-fry steamed dried scallops for about 1 minute until crisp and brown.

5. Dish out and garnish with crisp dried scallops and chives.

NOTE Cook the eggs lightly, so they retain their moisture. Overcooked eggs will be dry.

Steamed Fragrant Rice with Minced Pork, Chinese Sausages & Mushrooms Serves 4

Minced pork shoulder *200 g (7 oz)*

Chinese sausage *1, diced*

Fresh shiitake mushrooms *8, diced*

Cooking oil *2 Tbsp*

Minced ginger *1 tsp*

Minced garlic *1 tsp*

Minced coriander (cilantro) stems *1 tsp*

Minced shallots *1 tsp*

Corn flour (cornstarch) *1/2 tsp, mixed with 2 tsp water*

Cooked long-grain rice *2 Chinese rice bowls*

Spring onion (scallion) *1, white part only, chopped*

SEASONING (COMBINED)

Chicken stock (page 159) *250 ml (8 fl oz / 1 cup)*

Yellow bean sauce *3 tsp*

Seafood sauce *3 tsp*

Sugar *1/2 tsp*

Oyster sauce *1 tsp*

Dark soy sauce *a dash*

Sichuan pepper oil (page 161) *a dash*

Chinese cooking wine (*hua diao*) *a dash*

1. Bring a large pot of water to the boil. Put pork shoulder, sausages and mushrooms into a strainer and dip into hot water for about 10 seconds. Drain and set aside.

2. Heat oil in a wok and add ginger, garlic, coriander and shallots and stir-fry until fragrant. Add pork, sausage and mushrooms, then ingredients for seasoning. Bring to the boil and stir in corn flour mixture to thicken sauce.

3. Scoop cooked rice into serving bowls and spoon pork mixture over. Garnish with spring onion and serve hot.

Steamed Glutinous Rice with Crab

Serves 4

Glutinous rice *200 g (7 oz)*

Cooking oil *3 Tbsp*

Dried prawns (shrimps) *1 Tbsp,*
   soaked for 10 minutes, then
   drained and minced

Fresh shiitake mushrooms *2,*
   minced

Whole crabs *2, each about 250 g*
   (9 oz) each, chopped and washed

Homemade soy sauce (page 160)
   2 Tbsp

Chives *a small handful, chopped*

Crispy minced garlic (page 161)
   1 tsp

SEASONING (COMBINED)
Oyster sauce *2 tsp*

Light soy sauce *1 tsp*

Sesame oil *a dash*

Honey *$1/8$ tsp*

Minced garlic *2 tsp*

Ground white pepper *a dash*

Chinese cooking wine (*hua diao*)
   a dash

1. Start preparations a day ahead.

2. Soak glutinous rice in water overnight. The following day, drain rice, then place into an oiled steaming tray and steam for 45 minutes until rice is soft and sticky.

3. Meanwhile, prepare crabs. Pull off top shells and clean crabs. Chop into pieces, then rinse and drain well.

4. Heat 1 Tbsp oil in a wok. Add dried prawns and stir-fry until crisp and fragrant. Add mushrooms and stir-fry lightly. Pour mixture onto glutinous rice together with ingredients for seasoning. Mix well.

5. Transfer rice to a heatproof serving plate and place crabs on rice. Steam for 5 minutes until crabs are cooked.

6. Heat remaining 2 Tbsp oil in a wok and spoon over crabs. Do the same with homemade soy sauce. Garnish with chives and crispy minced garlic. Serve hot.

Malaysian-style Noodles with XO Sauce Serves 4

Flat yellow noodles *400 g (14¹/₃ oz)*

Cooking oil *2 Tbsp*

Dried sole powder (page 28) *1 tsp*

Fresh shiitake mushrooms *5, thinly sliced*

Crispy whole garlic (page 161) *1 Tbsp*

Chinese flowering cabbage (*cai xin*) *200 g (7 oz)*

STOCK

Chicken stock (page 159) *800 ml (27 fl oz)*

XO sauce *1 Tbsp*

Oyster sauce *2 tsp*

Dark soy sauce *a dash*

Sugar *¹/₂ tsp*

Ground white pepper *a dash*

1. Bring a pot of water to the boil over high heat. Blanch noodles for 20 seconds. Remove using a wire strainer and set aside.

2. Heat oil in a wok over medium heat. Add dried sole powder and stir-fry until fragrant.

3. Add mushrooms and crispy whole garlic together with all the ingredients for the stock.

4. Add noodles and cook over low heat for 3 minutes. Remove to a serving plate.

5. Bring a pot of water to the boil and add some oil and a pinch of salt. Briefly blanch Chinese flowering cabbage and drain. Place on top of noodles and serve immediately.

Wok-fried Vermicelli with Crab Serves 4

Crabs *2, each about 500 g (1 lb 1¹/₂ oz)*

Cooking oil *for deep-frying*

Ginger *10 slices*

Crispy whole garlic (page 161) *1 Tbsp*

Spring onion (scallion) *1, cut in short lengths*

White hon shimeji mushrooms *80 g (3 oz)*

Dried thin rice vermicelli *300 g (11 oz), soaked in water for 30 minutes, then drained*

STOCK (COMBINED)

Chicken stock (page 159) *800 ml (27 fl oz)*

Oyster sauce *2 tsp*

Salt *¹/₈ tsp*

Sugar *1 tsp*

Sesame oil *¹/₂ tsp*

Ground white pepper *a pinch*

Chinese cooking wine (*hua diao*) *a dash*

1. Prepare crabs. Pull off the top shells of crabs and clean. Cut off the pincers and cut the body into quarters.

2. Heat oil for deep-frying and deep-fry crabs for about 1 minute. Drain and set aside.

3. Heat 3 Tbsp oil in a wok and add ginger, crispy whole garlic, spring onion, mushrooms and crabs. Stir-fry until fragrant.

4. Add ingredients for stock and bring to the boil. Add vermicelli and stir-fry until sauce is thick.

5. Dish out and serve immediately.

Fish Head Noodles Serves 4

Fresh thick rice vermicelli)
  400 g (14¹/₃ oz)

Cooking oil *for deep-frying*

Snakehead fish or any white,
  firm-flesh fish *200 g (7 oz),
  chopped into pieces*

Pickled mustard cabbage
  (*zha cai*) *200 g (7 oz),
  cut into strips*

Ginger *5 slices*

Spring onions (scallions) *2, cut into
  short lengths*

Tomatoes *2, cut into wedges*

Lettuce *a few leaves*

Red chilli *1*

Light sauce soy *2 Tbsp*

STOCK

Chicken stock (page 159) *800 ml
  (27 fl oz)*

Salt *¹/₂ tsp*

Sugar *¹/₂ tsp*

Salted plum *1*

Ground white pepper *a dash*

Chinese cooking wine (*hua diao*)
  a dash

Sesame oil *a dash*

Milk *3 Tbsp*

1. Bring a pot of water to the boil and blanch noodles until soft.
   Drain well and place into a large serving bowl. Set aside.

2. Heat oil for deep-frying over high heat. Deep-fry fish head for about 2
   minutes until crisp and golden brown. Drain and set aside.

3. Heat 1 Tbsp oil in a wok and add ingredients for stock, except milk. Bring
   to the boil, then add fish head, pickled mustard cabbage, ginger, spring
   onions, tomatoes and milk.

4. Allow stock to return to the boil, then ladle into bowl over noodles.
   Garnish with lettuce and serve immediately with a saucer of cut red
   chillies in light soy sauce.

My Grandmother's Handmade Noodles Serves 4

Minced pork shoulder *200 g (7 oz)*

Fresh shiitake mushrooms *5, diced*

Cooking oil *2 Tbsp*

Minced garlic *1/2 tsp*

Corn flour (cornstarch) *1 1/2 tsp, mixed with 1 Tbsp water*

Crisp-fried shallots

DOUGH

Plain (all-purpose) flour *500 g (1 lb 1 1/2 oz)*

Water *180 ml (6 fl oz / 3/4 cup)*

Egg *1*

Salt *1/2 tsp*

Corn oil *1 Tbsp*

SEASONING (COMBINED)

Chicken stock (page 159) *150 ml (5 fl oz / 10 Tbsp)*

Oyster sauce *1 Tbsp*

Dark soy sauce *1/2 tsp*

Light soy sauce *1/2 Tbsp*

Sesame oil *a dash*

Chinese cooking wine (*hua diao*) *a dash*

Sugar *1/2 tsp*

STOCK

Cooking oil *2 Tbsp*

Dried white bait *2 Tbsp, rinsed*

Chicken stock (page 159) *1 litre (32 fl oz / 4 cups)*

Salt *1 tsp*

Sugar *1 tsp*

Ground white pepper *a pinch*

1. Prepare dough. Mix flour, water, egg, salt and corn oil in a bowl. Cover and set aside for 1 hour.

2. When dough is fully rested, bring a pot of water to the boil. Using your hands, pull out small pieces of dough, about 3 x 3-cm (1 x 1-in), and drop into pot. Cook for 2 minutes until dough floats to the surface. Remove cooked dough with a strainer and set aside.

3. Bring a fresh pot of water to the boil. Put pork and mushrooms into a strainer and dip into hot water to cook for 1–2 minutes. Drain and set aside.

4. Heat oil in a wok. Add minced garlic and stir-fry until fragrant. Add pork and mushrooms and stir-fry lightly, then add ingredients for seasoning. Bring to the boil and stir in corn flour mixture to thicken sauce.

5. Prepare stock. Heat oil in a wok over medium heat. Add white bait and stir-fry until lightly brown and fragrant. Add chicken stock, salt, sugar and pepper. Bring to the boil, then add cooked dough. Lower heat and simmer for 2 minutes. Ladle into bowls.

6. Spoon pork mixture over noodles, or serve on the side with noodles. Garnish with crisp-fried shallots and serve immediately.

Snacks & Desserts

Glutinous Rice Flour Dumplings with Red Dates,
   Longan & Lotus Seeds in Syrup 142

Glutinous Rice Flour Dumplings in Almond Cream 144

Sweet Potatoes in Ginger Syrup 146

Stuffed Red Dates 148

Double-boiled Nashi Pear with Hashima & Ginseng 150

Warm Pumpkin Cream Brûlée 152

Glutinous Rice Flour Dumplings with Red Dates, Longan & Lotus Seeds in Syrup Serves 4

Dried lotus seeds *100 g (3¹/₂ oz)*

Dried gingko nuts *100 g (3¹/₂ oz)*

Chinese red dates *20*

Dried longan *100 g (3¹/₂ oz)*

Water *1 litre (32 fl oz / 4 cups)*

Rock sugar *200 g (7 oz)*

Sterculia seed (*pang da hai*) *1*

Frozen glutinous rice flour balls with peanut or sesame filling *3–4 per person*

Mint leaves

1. Prepare lotus seeds and gingko nuts. Soak them in warm water for 30 minutes. Use a wooden skewer to push the bitter shoot out from lotus seeds and gingko nuts.

2. Put lotus seeds, gingko nuts, red dates, longan, water and rock sugar into the inner pot of a double-boiler and steam for 2 hours. If you do not have a double-boiler, place the ingredients into a heatproof pot, cover and steam for 2 hours.

3. Meanwhile, soak sterculia seed in a small bowl of water for 30 minutes until the flesh expands into a jelly-like mass. Peel off and discard the skin.

4. When the syrup is ready, bring a pot of water to the boil and cook dumplings for 5 minutes until they float. Drain and divide among 4 serving bowls.

5. Ladle syrup with some red dates, longan, lotus seeds and gingko nuts over dumplings. Top with sterculia seed and garnish with mint. Serve immediately.

Glutinous Rice Flour Dumplings in Almond Cream Serves 4

Sweet apricot kernels
  1 kg (2 lb 3 oz)

Bitter apricot kernels
  500 g (1 lb 1 1/2 oz)

Thai fragrant rice *300 g (11 oz)*

Water *6 litres (192 fl oz / 24 cups)*

Almond powder *1 Tbsp*

Whipping cream *200 ml (7 fl oz)*

Sugar *100 g (3 1/2 oz) or to taste*

Sterculia seed (*pang da hai*) 1

Frozen glutinous rice flour balls
  with black sesame filling *3–4 per
  person*

Hawaiian papaya *1/4, small, peeled
  and seeded, cut into cubes*

Mint leaves

1. Start preparations a day ahead. Soak apricot kernels and rice in 6 litres (192 fl oz / 24 cups) water and leave overnight.

2. The following day, blend apricot kernels and rice together with the soaking liquid into a fine purée. Do this in batches. Pour purée into a clean muslin cloth or new cloth coffee strainer and squeeze to extract milk into a pot. Discard pulp.

3. Stir almond powder, whipping cream and sugar into almond milk and bring to the boil. The resulting almond cream should be slightly thick, like evaporated milk. If it is too watery, stir in 1/2 tsp corn flour, mixed first with 2 tsp water to thicken it.

4. Soak sterculia seed in a small bowl of water for 30 minutes until the flesh expands into a jelly-like mass. Peel off and discard the skin.

5. Bring a pot of water to the boil and cook dumplings for 5 minutes until they float. Remove with slotted spoon and divide among 4 serving bowls.

6. Blend papaya with an equal amount of water into a purée.

7. Ladle almond cream over dumplings. Drizzle with papaya purée and garnish with sterculia seed and mint leaves. Serve immediately.

Sweet Potatoes in Ginger Syrup Serves 4

Variety of sweet potatoes *500 g (1 lb 1¹/₂ oz), scrubbed clean*

GINGER SYRUP

Chinese red dates *20*

Dried longans *100 g (3¹/₂ oz)*

Young ginger *5-cm (2-in) knob, peeled*

Water *2 litres (64 fl oz / 8 cups)*

Rock sugar *200 g (7 oz) or to taste*

1. Put all ingredients for ginger syrup into the inner pot of a double-boiler and steam for 2 hours. If you do not have a double-boiler, place the ingredients into a heatproof pot, cover and steam for 2 hours. Strain syrup.

2. Meanwhile, put sweet potatoes into a steamer and steam for 30–45 minutes until sweet potatoes are soft. Cut into bite-size pieces and divide among 4 serving bowls.

3. Ladle ginger syrup over sweet potatoes and serve.

Stuffed Red Dates Serves 4

Chinese red dates *20*

Glutinous rice flour *100 g (3¹/₂ oz)*

Water *2 Tbsp*

Cooking oil *for deep-frying*

Osmanthus blossoms (optional)
1 tsp

THICK SUGAR SYRUP

Water *500 ml (16 fl oz / 2 cups)*

Rock sugar *1 kg (2 lb 3 oz)*

1. Start preparations a day ahead. Leave Chinese red dates to soak in water overnight.

2. The following day, start by preparing sugar syrup. Put water and sugar into a pot and simmer over medium heat for 20 minutes, stirring occasionally, until syrup is thick like honey.

3. Meanwhile, mix glutinous rice flour with 2 Tbsp water into dough. Add more water if necessary. Roll dough into a cylindrical shape and cut into 20 equal pieces. Shape dough into ovals the size of red dates.

4. Drain dates and make a slit down the length of each one. Stuff each date with a ball of dough.

5. Heat oil for deep-frying over medium heat. Lower dates into hot oil and deep-fry until dough is lightly golden. Remove dates from oil.

6. Bring a pot of water to the boil and blanch dates in hot water for 1 minute to remove the oil.

7. Place stuffed dates into sugar syrup and simmer for 1 minute. Dish out and garnish with osmanthus blossoms, if desired. Serve.

Double-boiled Nashi Pear with Hashima & Ginseng Serves 4

Dried hashima 20 g (²/₃ oz)

Hot water 550 ml (18 fl oz / 2¹/₄ cups)

Ginger 1 slice

Dried ginseng 10 g (¹/₃ oz), rinsed

Nashi pears 3

Chinese red dates 20

Dried longans 100 g (3¹/₂ oz)

Water 1 litre (32 fl oz / 4 cups)

Rock sugar 200 g (7 oz) or to taste

GARNISH

Chinese wolfberries 1 tsp, soaked in water for 10 minutes

Mint leaves

1. Start preparations a day ahead. Leave hashima to soak in water overnight.

2. The following day, drain hashima, then remove any dirt or impurities. Put cleaned hashima into a heatproof bowl with 500 ml (16 fl oz / 2 cups) hot water and a slice of ginger. Place ginseng into another heatproof bowl with remaining hot water. Place bowls in a steamer and steam hashima for 10 minutes and ginseng for 30 minutes.

3. Cut pears in half and use a melon baller to scoop out as many rounds as possible from pears. Discard core and skin.

4. Put pears, dates, longans, water and sugar into a steaming bowl and steam for 1 hour. Remove and discard dates and longans. Divide pears and syrup among 4 serving bowls.

5. Add hashima and ginseng to bowls. Garnish with Chinese wolfberries and mint leaves. Serve hot or refrigerate and serve cold.

Warm Pumpkin Cream Brûlée Serves 4

PUMPKIN BRÛLÉE

Butternut pumpkin *100 g (3¹/₂ oz), peeled and cut into cubes*

Eggs *2*

Egg yolks *2*

Sugar *50 g (1²/₃ oz) + more for sprinkling*

Whipping cream *400 ml (14 fl oz / 1²/₃ cups)*

GARNISH (OPTIONAL)

Mixed berries

Mint leaves

Icing (confectioner's) sugar

1. Put pumpkin into a steamer and steam for 30 minutes until pumpkin is soft. Mash pumpkin in a mixing bowl.

2. Preheat the oven to 170°C (330°F).

3. Add all remaining ingredients for brûlée to mashed pumpkin in mixing bowl and mix until sugar is melted. Strain mixture.

4. Pour mixture into 4 small heatproof dishes and place into a deep baking tray. Pour enough hot water into tray to come halfway up the sides of dishes. Place tray into the oven and bake for 40–50 minutes until brûlée is set. Remove from the oven.

5. Sprinkle some sugar on top of each dish of cream brûlée. Use a kitchen torch to melt and burn sugar to form a thin crust. Alternatively, place under a grill.

6. Garnish with mixed berries, mint leaves and icing sugar, if desired. Serve.

Basic
Recipes

The following recipes are for stocks,
sauces and condiments that are used
frequently in Chinese cooking.

It is advisable to prepare a batch of each recipe and store
it as advised in the individual recipes for use whenever it is
needed. Once you are familiar with the taste and flavours of
these basic stocks, sauces and condiments, you can also use
them to perk up your own recipes!

CHICKEN STOCK

Makes about 3 litres (96 fl oz / 12 cups)

Chicken stock can be prepared ahead of time and kept refrigerated for up to 3 days or frozen for up to 1 month. Alternatively, ready-made chicken stock packed into cartons can be purchased from most supermarkets. If using ready-made chicken stock, look for those without added seasoning.

Water *5 litres (160 fl oz / 20 cups)*

Chicken *1, about 1 kg (2 lb 3 oz)*

Chicken feet *1 kg (2lb 3 oz)*

Lean pork *1 kg (2 lb 3 oz)*

Chinese (Yunnan) ham *350 g (12 oz)*

1. Bring water to the boil in a pot and add chicken, chicken feet, lean pork and ham. Simmer over low heat for 5 hours, or until about 3 litres (96 fl oz / 12 cups) stock is left in the pot.

2. Strain stock before using.

STEAMED DRIED SCALLOPS

Prepares 20 scallops

Like homemade chicken stock, steamed dried scallops take time to prepare, so cook up a large batch and keep refrigerated for up to 1 week.

Dried scallops *20, medium*

Chicken stock (page 159) *as needed*

Salt *1/4 tsp*

Ginger *2 slices*

Spring onion (scallion) *1, chopped*

Cooking oil *1 tsp*

1. Soak dried scallops in water and leave for 2 hours.

2. Drain dried scallops and put into a steaming bowl. Add enough chicken stock to cover scallops, then add salt, ginger, spring onion and cooking oil. Put into a steamer and steam for 45 minutes.

3. Use the dried scallops together with the liquid.

PICKLED RED CHILLIES

Makes about 2 cups

Pickled red chilli is available in jars from some supermarkets. If unavailable, you can make your own using this recipe. Pickled red chillies can be stored in a clean container in the refrigerator indefinitely.

Red chillies *400 g (14^1/$_3$ oz), stalks removed*

White vinegar *80 ml (2^1/$_2$ fl oz / ^{1}/$_3$ cup)*

Salt *2 Tbsp*

Ginger *4 slices*

1. Start preparations a week ahead.

2. Chop chillies finely. Do not use a blender or the chillies will not keep. Transfer to a plastic bottle with a screw cap and add vinegar, salt and ginger. Leave at room temperature for 7 days. This will rid the chillies of their spiciness.

3. Use as needed.

HOMEMADE SOY SAUCE

Makes about *100 ml (3^1/$_2$ fl oz)*

Although similar in appearance to light soy sauce, this homemade soy sauce is highly fragrant due to the use of ginger, spring onion and coriander. Make up a larger batch and keep it in a clean jar for use whenever you need it.

Cooking oil *^{1}/$_2$ Tbsp*

Ginger *2 slices*

Spring onion (scallion) *1, cut into short lengths*

Coriander leaves (cilantro) *2 sprigs*

Chicken stock (page 159) *100 ml (3^1/$_2$ fl oz)*

Light soy sauce *1 Tbsp*

Dark soy sauce *a dash*

Rock sugar *10 g (3^1/$_2$ oz)*

1. Heat oil in a wok and stir-fry ginger, spring onion and coriander until fragrant. Add remaining ingredients and bring to the boil.

2. Strain and use as needed.

CRISPY MINCED GARLIC

Makes about 3 Tbsp

Crispy minced garlic will keep in a clean airtight container for up to 1 week.

Garlic *3 heads, peeled*

Cooking oil *for deep-frying*

1. Mince garlic and rinse, then place in a strainer to drain well.

2. Heat oil for deep-frying over medium heat. Add minced garlic and cook in batches for about 2 minutes until garlic is brown and crisp. Remove and drain well.

3. Use as needed.

CRISPY WHOLE GARLIC

Prepares 3 heads of garlic

Crispy whole garlic will keep in a clean airtight container for up to 1 week.

Garlic *3 heads, peeled*

Cooking oil *for deep-frying*

1. Rinse garlic and place in a strainer to drain well.

2. Heat oil for deep-frying over medium heat. Add garlic and cook in batches for about 2 minutes until garlic is brown and crisp. Remove and drain well.

3. Use as needed.

SICHUAN PEPPER

Makes about 1 Tbsp

Like Sichuan pepper oil, Sichuan pepper will add a distinctive spicy flavour to dishes. As only a small pinch is needed to flavour a dish, this amount will last for some time.

Sichuan pepper *1 Tbsp*

1. Preheat oven to 70°C (155°F) and toast Sichuan pepper for 10 minutes.

2. Remove and pound with a mortar and pestle or grind using a pepper mill.

3. Use as needed.

SICHUAN PEPPER OIL

Makes about 100 ml (3^1/$_2$ fl oz)

Sichuan pepper oil will add a distinctive spicy flavour to dishes. As only a few drops are needed to flavour a dish, this amount will last for some time.

Corn oil *100 ml (3^1/$_2$ fl oz)*

Sichuan pepper *50 g (1^2/$_3$ oz)*

1. Put oil and Sichuan pepper in a wok and cook over medium heat for about 10 minutes until the smell of the oil is apparent.

2. Strain oil and store in a clean glass jar.

3. Use as needed.

Glossary

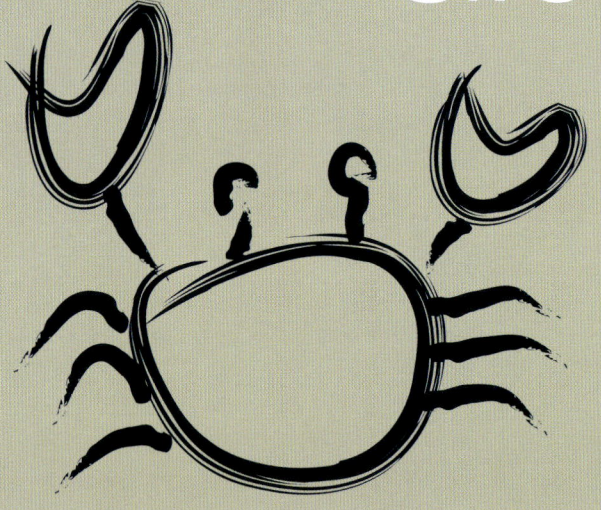

AMERICAN GINSENG

Also known as *yang shen* (Chinese) or *yong sam* (Cantonese), ginseng is believed to invigorate the body and encourage healing after illness. There are many grades of ginseng, so feel free to exercise your options of using a grade of ginseng that suits your budget.

ANGLED LUFFA

Angled luffas belong to the melon family. They have stiff longitudinal ridges and are typically 30–60-cm (12–24 in) in length. Select dark green and thin melons, as these tend to be younger. Older melons may sometimes be bitter.

BLACK FUNGUS

Also known as wood ear fungus, black fungus is sold dried and must be reconstituted by soaking in water. Once softened, cut away any hard woody bits and discard. Although bland with no taste of its own, black fungus is enjoyed for its crunchy texture. It is typically sliced and added to stir-fries, soups or stews.

DRIED SCALLOPS

Also known as conpoy, these dried sea scallops are available in various sizes and vary in quality. They have a strong flavour and are usually added to steamed or stewed dishes. Dried scallops will keep indefinitely if stored in a clean airtight container in a cool, dry place.

DRIED SOLE

This dried fillet of sole fish has a fragrant aroma and is used for flavouring dishes. Bake, then grind or pound to use as a powder.

GINGKO NUTS

Gingko nuts are sold shelled or still in their light brown shells. Unshelled nuts need to be cracked, then soaked to remove the brown skin. Fresh, shelled nuts are available in some supermarkets, but they require refrigeration and have a shelf life of only a few weeks. To prepare shelled gingko nuts, push a toothpick or skewer through one tapered end of the nut to remove the bitter core. A good alternative is canned gingko nuts, which come pre-prepared, with the bitter core already removed.

FERMENTED BEAN CURD (FU YU)

Also known as preserved bean curd or bean curd cheese, fermented bean curd is aged in brine and flavoured with chilli. It has a pungent flavour and a dense but smooth and creamy texture, not unlike soft cheese. It can be eaten as is with porridge, or used as a condiment or flavouring. Fermented bean curd is sold in jars.

GLUTEN

A meat substitute common in Asian vegetarian diets, gluten is made from wheat flour dough with the starch washed away. It is high in protein with a chewy texture not unlike meat. It is available in vacuum packs or cans.

HASHIMA

Also known as hasma, *xue ge* (Chinese) or *shuet kup* (Cantonese), hashima is the gland of a species of frog. Dried hashima looks like brown flakes or crumbs, and must be reconstituted by soaking. When reconstituted, hashima looks like clumps of cloudy, translucent jelly. Pick out any traces of dirt or impurities before using.

LILY BULBS

Fresh lily bulbs are pearly white in colour and look like small garlic bulbs. To use, rinse, then peel off the petals. Fresh lily bulbs have a crisp texture and sweet taste and can be eaten as is, or lightly cooked in stir-fries or sweet desserts.

OSMANTHUS BLOSSOMS

Also known as *gui hua* (Chinese), these small dried yellow flowers have a light floral fragrance and are typically used to flavour teas or Chinese desserts, and sometimes used as a garnish. Osmanthus blossoms can be purchased from Chinese herbal stores.

PICKLED BAMBOO SHOOT

The young shoot of the bamboo plant, bamboo shoot is available fresh, dried or preserved in cans and jars. It has a mild flavour and crunchy texture and can be added to stir-fries and soups. In this book, pickled bamboo shoot is used for its taste and convenience. It is available in jars, already cut into strips and needs no other preparation.

PRESERVED CHILLI

These are minced red chillies preserved in vinegar. The vinegar removes the hotness of the chillies, leaving just a mouthwatering tangy flavour, making it ideal for seasoning bland foods like fish.

PICKLED RED BELL PEPPERS

Also known as sweet cherry peppers, these are baby bell peppers (capsicums) that have been pickled in a solution of salt, vinegar and water. It is very tasty and can be added to simple stir-fries to perk up the dish.

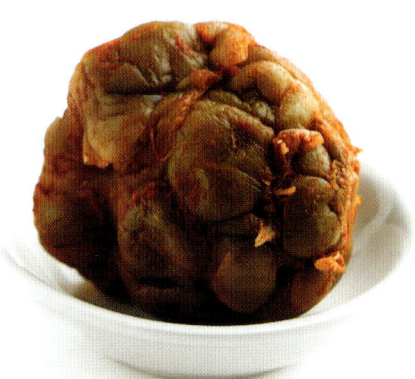

SOY BEAN CRUMB

Known better by its Chinese name, *dou so*, this is a product from Taiwan. It is made from soy beans that are dry-roasted and chopped, then compressed into a ball. It is available from the dry goods store in some markets.

SICHUAN PICKLED CABBAGE

Also know as *zha cai* (Chinese) or *harm choy* (Cantonese), this pickled mustard stem is a combination of spicy and salty flavours. It has a crunchy texture and is enjoyed in Chinese cold dishes, soups or stir-fries. To remove the salty flavour, soak the cut vegetable in water for 10–15 minutes before cooking.

STERCULIA SEEDS

Also known as *pang da hai* (Chinese) or *dai hau lam* (Cantonese), sterculia seeds are available from Chinese herbal shops. They are sold dried and expand when soaked in water. The resulting jelly-like mass has no flavour of its own, but is enjoyed for its texture. It is typically added to sweet desserts.

WHITE BAIT

Sometimes also known as silver fish, these white-coloured anchovies are available both fresh and dried. They are different from the more common dried anchovies (*ikan bilis*) and have a finer texture. They are also sweeter in taste, but are similarly used to flavour soups or stir-fries.

YELLOW BEAN SAUCE

Also known as yellow or brown bean paste or fermented yellow soy bean paste, this salty condiment is sold in jars, with the beans whole or mashed. The whole beans can be mashed for greater flavour when cooking. Keep the paste refrigerated after opening and it will keep indefinitely.

Weights & Measures

Quantities for this book are given in Metric, Imperial and American (spoon) measures.
Standard spoon and cup measurements used are: 1 tsp = 5 ml, 1 Tbsp = 15 ml, 1 cup = 250 ml.
All measures are level unless otherwise stated.

LIQUID AND VOLUME MEASURES

Metric	Imperial	American
5 ml	1/6 fl oz	1 teaspoon
10 ml	1/3 fl oz	1 dessertspoon
15 ml	1/2 fl oz	1 tablespoon
60 ml	2 fl oz	1/4 cup (4 tablespoons)
85 ml	2 1/2 fl oz	1/3 cup
90 ml	3 fl oz	3/8 cup (6 tablespoons)
125 ml	4 fl oz	1/2 cup
180 ml	6 fl oz	3/4 cup
250 ml	8 fl oz	1 cup
300 ml	10 fl oz (1/2 pint)	1 1/4 cups
375 ml	12 fl oz	1 1/2 cups
435 ml	14 fl oz	1 3/4 cups
500 ml	16 fl oz	2 cups
625 ml	20 fl oz (1 pint)	2 1/2 cups
750 ml	24 fl oz (1 1/5 pints)	3 cups
1 litre	32 fl oz (1 3/5 pints)	4 cups
1.25 litres	40 fl oz (2 pints)	5 cups
1.5 litres	48 fl oz (2 2/5 pints)	6 cups
2.5 litres	80 fl oz (4 pints)	10 cups

DRY MEASURES

Metric	Imperial
30 grams	1 ounce
45 grams	1 1/2 ounces
55 grams	2 ounces
70 grams	2 1/2 ounces
85 grams	3 ounces
100 grams	3 1/2 ounces
110 grams	4 ounces
125 grams	4 1/2 ounces
140 grams	5 ounces
280 grams	10 ounces
450 grams	16 ounces (1 pound)
500 grams	1 pound, 1 1/2 ounces
700 grams	1 1/2 pounds
800 grams	1 3/4 pounds
1 kilogram	2 pounds, 3 ounces
1.5 kilograms	3 pounds, 4 1/2 ounces
2 kilograms	4 pounds, 6 ounces

OVEN TEMPERATURE

	°C	°F	Gas Regulo
Very slow	120	250	1
Slow	150	300	2
Moderately slow	160	325	3
Moderate	180	350	4
Moderately hot	190/200	370/400	5/6
Hot	210/220	410/440	6/7
Very hot	230	450	8
Super hot	250/290	475/550	9/10

LENGTH

Metric	Imperial
0.5 cm	1/4 inch
1 cm	1/2 inch
1.5 cm	3/4 inch
2.5 cm	1 inch